MYTHS OF IDAHO INDIANS

MYTHS OF IDAHO INDIANS

DEWARD E. WALKER, JR.

ILLUSTRATED BY
TERRY ARMSTRONG

UNIVERSITY OF IDAHO PRESS
MOSCOW, IDAHO

© 1980 by The University of Idaho.
An Anthropological Monograph of the University of Idaho,
Roderick Sprague, editor

Printed in the United States of America
93   92   91   5

Library of Congress Catalog
Card number 79-57484

ISBN 0-89301-066-9

Table of Contents

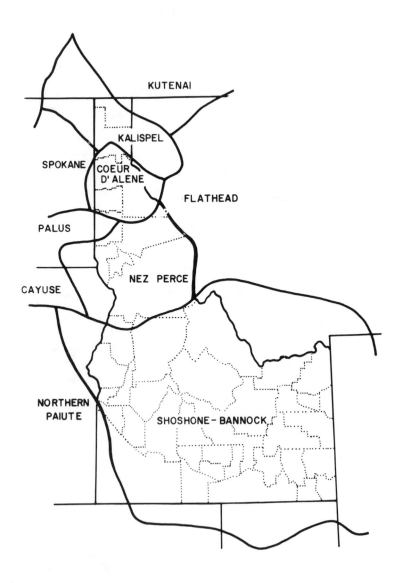

Indian Tribes of Idaho

INTRODUCTION

All societies have prose literary forms, whether oral or written. In aboriginal Idaho, as in many parts of the world, this takes the form of myths, or as they are often termed, legends. We have included our discussion on mythology with the analysis of religion because the two are closely related in many ways. Myths impart the basic values and beliefs of a society and give moral instruction to its members. They serve to explain the creation of the world and its beings, the significance of rituals and customs, and the religious meaning of birth, death, and other natural occurrences. In one sense the Christian Bible is a similar set of myths which impart basic religious truths.

In addition to their explanatory function, myths also serve as mechanisms for educating children, stimulating social interaction, and amusement. The behavior of animal characters instructs children in proper behavior and teaches them lessons of practical value, such as the habits of game animals, the location of food resources, how to use tools and implements, and the geography of their territory. Myths frequently stimulate a sense of group cohesion and pride, because they describe how a people were created and often how they are superior to others.

In aboriginal Idaho, myths were usually recounted by elders during the winter and emphasized several recurrent themes. Some myths explained the origin of the present order, i.e., how an animal, topographical feature, or customary way of doing things came to be the way it was. Others demonstrated how clever deception and trickery could either help or hinder, depending on whether they were used for group welfare or in a selfish, egotistic manner. Lessons in the grievous results of theft, gluttony, and cheating of relatives were especially common in the myths. Contests of strength and endurance reflected the high value placed on physical fitness and courage. The need for group cohesion and cooperation against outside threats was also depicted in the conquest of ogres, monsters, and cannibals. Immanent justice, the belief that the right will triumph in the end, was frequently expressed in myths about revenge, justice, and the defeat of animal characters who acted against group welfare. As in myths everywhere, magic is frequently used for well-known purposes, mostly to make a good story better and to extricate characters in the stories from otherwise impossible situations. Magical loss and replacement of body parts, magical revival from the dead, and transformation of the self occur frequently in the myths. In the myths below, Coyote often uses magic to transform things into their present shape. Indeed, the central character in the mythology of most American Indians is a *transformer-trickster*, who changes himself, other animals, people, and topographical features in various ways. Countless myths from aboriginal Idaho recall how Coyote, the principal trickster, changed an animal or natural object into its present form.

The trickster figure is a worldwide phenomenon, and has parallels in the picaresque novels of Spain, the fairy tales of the Brothers Grimm, Greek gods and goddesses, and the literary traditions of countless other cultures. The psychiatrist C.G. Jung (1956) provides a useful commentary on this figure:

> "He is . . . God, man, and animal at once. He is both subhuman and superhuman, a bestial and divine being . . . he is in many respects stupider than the animals, and gets into one ridiculous scrape after another. Although he is not really evil he does the most atrocious things. . . . The trickster is a primitive 'cosmic' being of 'divine-animal' nature, on the one hand superior to man because of his superhuman qualities, and on the other hand inferior to him because of his unreason. . . . He is no match for the animals either, because of his extraordinary clumsiness and lack of instinct. . . ."

In myths the trickster often acts out man's socially disruptive drives, thereby revealing the disastrous results of

8

violating conventional mores. There is an implication in most myths that man has progressed beyond this state of amorality and unreason to become a superior being. In fact, children are explicitly encouraged to learn how to behave properly from the clumsiness and foolishness of Coyote who lived before the people came in a time sometimes called the pre-cultural era.

The following selected myths from aboriginal Idaho expresses the rich spiritual and aesthetic side of these cultures. Material remains tell us something about the mundane, every-day aspects of life, but these oral traditions more adequately reflect the thoughts and values of this bygone era. In selecting and translating the myths, we have preserved as much of the original flavor and style as possible, but much of the dramatic quality and fun in the myths is apparent only when they are told in the native language. Therefore, we have attempted to preserve the narrative form in which the myths were originally told. In some cases the more risque elements have been deleted, either by the original storyteller or by those who recorded them. This unfortunate practice sometimes mars an otherwise delightfully humorous story. Finally, the reader is encouraged to interpret the myths in light of the cultural circumstances of the people who originated them. Unless their cultural context is considered, much of the meaning and context becomes unintelligible. With such precautions, however, we in the twentieth century can glimpse at least the dark outlines of a rich and exciting cultural world which only a handful of elderly Indians now remember.

Sources

Some might say that ethnology in Idaho begins with the observations of the first explorers, fur traders, missionaries, and government agents to enter the area. Although they sometimes made highly accurate observations, in most cases these writings lack accuracy and comprehension. Although there are exceptions, they usually present a prejudiced, naive, ethnocentric viewpoint, wherein the writer sees his own Euro-

American culture as vastly superior to the native cultures. Many of the earlier writings of ethnologists are also inadequate and lack the insights of more recent works. Thus, caution must be exercised when drawing on many published materials dealing with the native peoples of Idaho and American Indians in general.

A number of highly reliable ethnological works on aboriginal American Indians have become available in recent years. These deal with the United States and North America as a whole, although most contain some useful materials on Idaho. References to them are included in the references cited. Driver (1961), Murdock (1960, 1967), Spencer, Jennings, et al. (1965), Oswalt (1966), Underhill (1953, 1965), Walker (1971), and Eggan (1955) probably are the best general reference works now available. Swanson (1970) has edited a useful book on native cultures of the Northwest. Published ethnological works on the aboriginal cultures of Idaho are much more difficult to obtain. Many are either out of print or published in journals not usually available in local libraries. However, most can be obtained by your local librarian, thanks to the interlibrary loan program. If the original sources are to be consulted, this procedure is required.

The most comprehensive general ethnography on the Kutenai is by Turney-High (1941). This ethnography includes information on Kutenai history and intergroup relations, natural environment, technology and subsistence activities, housing, transportation, clothing, individual life cycle, family and political organization, art, and religion. Baker (1955) briefly covers the same topics as Turney-High and adds substantial materials on acculturation and present conditions. Jenness (1932) covers most of the material contained in Turney-High and Baker, but only superficially. Additional notes on the Kutenai will be found in the many earlier publications of the pioneers Wilson (1890) and Chamberlain (1893, 1893-95, 1894, 1901a, 1901b, 1901c, 1902, 1905, 1907, 1909). Ray (1942) wrote a useful ethnographic summary on the Kutenai, and Boas (1918) is the major source on Kutenai mythology. Ewers (1955) makes occasional comments on Kutenai horse culture.

10

The principal published ethnography on the Kalispel is by James Teit (1930). He describes them as part of what he calls the "Flathead Group" which includes the Flathead, Pend d'Oreille, and Kalispel. Information is included on their history and intergroup relations, natural environment, technology and subsistence activities, housing, transportation, clothing, individual life cycles, family and political organization, art, and religion. An interesting master's thesis containing information on Kalispel kinship and family organization was written by Bahar (1955). Ray (1942) also summarizes most of the available ethnographic information on the Kalispel, and Teit (1917a, 1917b) and Vogt (1940) are major sources on Kalispel mythology.

James Teit (1930) described the Coeur d'Alene with much the same ethnographic information he presents for the Kalispel. The master's theses of Dozier (1961) and Stevens (1955) also contain much useful information. Gladys Reichard (1930, 1947) and James Teit (1917a) have published extensively on Coeur d'Alene myths, and Ewers (1955) presents some information on the uses of the horse among the Coeur d'Alene. Ray (1942) has given us a useful ethnographic summary of this group.

Most readers will know the Nez Perces through historians such as Haines (1938, 1955) and Josephy (1965). Fortunately, an increasing number of ethnologists are turning their attention to the Nez Perces. Lundsgaarde (1963) describes kinship and family organization, and Schwede (1970) concentrates on settlement patterns. Spinden (1908) presents information covered in traditional ethnographies —natural environment, technology and subsistence activities, housing, transportation, clothing, individual life cycles, family and political organization, art, and religion. Walker (1964, 1966, 1967a, 1967b, 1968a, 1968b) adds to Spinden's observations on political organization, religion, subsistence and technology, and Ewers (1955) presents some valuable information on Nez Perce horse culture. We are particularly fortunate in having a large number of published Nez Perce myths by a Nez Perce anthropologist, Archie Phinney (1934).

Robert Lowie (1909, 1915, 1919, 1924a, 1924b) is a major

11

contributor to the ethnography of the aboriginal Shoshone-Bannock, providing information on territory, technology and subsistence activities, family and political organization, religion, art, and mythology. Julian Steward (1936, 1938a, 1938b, 1955) also provides extensive ethnographic information on the Northern Shoshone and many other groups in the Great Basin. Steward concentrates particularly on environment, subsistence and technology, population density, settlement patterns, and family and political organization. More recently, Cappannari (1950) has summarized and interpreted the information dealing with property concepts among the Shoshone. Similar information on the closely allied Bannock will be found in Steward (1938a) and Madsen (1948). Other useful sources are Downs (1966), Fowler (1966), Stewart (1966), and Swanson (1966), all of whom are included in the recent symposium on anthropological research in the Great Basin (d'Azevedo, et al. 1966). Ewers (1955) presents a limited amount of information on Shoshone-Bannock horse culture.

Omer Stewart (1937, 1939a, 1939b, 1941, 1944) has been a major contributor to Northern Paiute ethnography. His publications include information on territory, environment, subsistence activities, family and political organization, housing, clothing, transportation, and religion. His 1939a publication focuses primarily on political organization. Julian Steward (1938a) also deals with Northern Paiute environment, political and family organization, technology and subsistence activities, and population. Another very important contributor is Whiting (1950) who concentrates on the Harney Valley division of the Northern Paiute. Although she heavily emphasizes religion, social control, and sorcery, she also includes much information on the individual life cycle and subsistence activities. Willard Park (1937) also focuses on Northern Paiute religion, and Ruth Underhill (1941) gives a general summary of the aboriginal ethnography of the Northern Paiute. Isabel Kelly (1938) is a good source for Northern Paiute myths.

About the Author

Esther David is an Indian Jewish author and illustrator belonging to the Bene Israel Jewish community of Ahmedabad. Her novel, *Book of Rachel*, received the Sahitya Akademi Award for English literature in 2010. She has received the Hadassah-Brandeis Institute Research Award, USA, for the study of Indian Jewish cuisine.

Kutenai Myths

14

The Youth Who Killed The Chiefs

An old man and his wife and their daughter lived in a tent. A chief came to see them and the daughter married him. They had a male child whom the chief killed. The woman continued living in the tent and had a girl child. The chief stayed with her and hunted game. One day he killed and skinned a buffalo cow. He put the meat on a travois and started back to the tent. When he arrived he did not give any meat to his parents-in-law, and the old woman was hungry.

The old man's daughter had another child, a male. She said to her father, "Do not tell the chief that I have given birth. Early tomorrow shoot a buffalo cow and don't be afraid of the chief." Early the next day the old man shot and killed a buffalo cow. The chief went out and saw the old man skinning it. He went into the tent and took a bow thinking, "I will kill that old man." He approached the old man and said, "Did you kill a cow?" The old man replied, "Yes, it is mine." The chief said, "No, it is not yours, it is mine." The chief readied his bow to kill the old man but did not see his son who was there. The youth arose, took his bow, and shot and killed the chief. The youth said to his grandfather, "Now take the meat and go back home." The boy went to the chief's tent, killed the chief's other wives, and threw them outside. He said to his grandfather, "Go in, it shall be your tent."

The boy then asked his mother, "Are there any other people?" She said, "There is a town down the river and the chief there is like this one because he does not give away food." The youth said, "I will go there." When he arrived there he entered an old woman's tent. He said to her, "I am hungry," and she replied, "We are hungry." She then took a dish, put something into it, and gave it to him. Again the youth said, "I am hungry," and the old woman said. "We are hungry too. There is much food in the chief's tent, but nobody goes in there." The youth said, "I'll go." Even though the old woman warned him against it, the boy went to the chief's tent. The chief was asleep. The youth awoke him saying, "I have entered your tent." The chief got up from his bed and became a rattlesnake. The youth took his arrow, struck the chief and shot him down. The chief's wives became rattlesnakes, and the youth shot them down. He went out and said, "Come in, all of you, and get some meat."

The youth again asked, "Are there no other people?" He was told, "There is another town down the river, but the chief is bad." He went to that town and entered an old woman's tent. He said to her, "I am hungry," and she answered, "We are hungry." She took a dish, put something into it, and gave it to him. He said to her, "I said I am hungry." He was told, "There is no food. There is much food in the chief's tent, but nobody goes in there." The youth said, "I'll go." He entered and found the chief asleep. He said to him, "Get up." The chief got up from his bed and became a grizzly bear. The youth took his arrow and shot him down. At once the chief's wives became grizzly bears and the youth shot them down. Then he threw them outside and said, "Take the meat." The people took the meat.

The youth said, "Are there no other people?" He was told, "There is a town down the river." He went to that town and entered an old woman's tent. He said to her, "I am hungry," and was told, "We have no food." She took a dish, put something into it and gave it to him. He said to her again, "I am hungry," and was told, "There is much food in that tent, but nobody goes in there." The youth said, "I'll go." He was told by the old woman, "Don't go there," but he entered the chief's tent and sat down. He said to the chief, "Arise." The chief got up from his bed and became a bull buffalo. The youth took his arrow and struck him down. The chief's wives at once became buffalo cows. The boy struck them down and threw them outside. Then he said, "Come and take the meat."

Coyote and Buffalo

Coyote was walking along when he found the head of a Buffalo Bull. He picked it up and threw it away, then he went on. He came back the same way where the Bull head was and threw it away again. When he passed there again it was still in the same place. This happened three times. Then he said to it, "When I went here before this is where you were lying, and you lie in the same place again." He took a stone and smashed the head and then scattered the pieces about. He found a flat stone and threw his blanket over it, then he laid down. While he was lying down, he cried out.

Coyote heard running noises. He arose and looked around, but there was nothing. "Oh, I thought I heard someone running; it was nothing but the passerby." He laid down again. After a little while he heard running noises again. He raised his head quickly and saw a Bull approaching. He jumped up quickly and started to run, but the Bull chased him. Soon he was out of breath and was tired. The Coyote spoke and said, "Somebody must help me," and a nearby voice said, "Nephew, come to me." Coyote disappeared inside a stump. The Bull knew that Coyote was in there, so he butted the tree and split it in two. Coyote ran away quickly. When he had gone a little ways, he was out of breath again, and he spoke again saying, "How far away are you manitou? I am in danger." He was told, "Nephew, come to me, come in." Coyote saw a stone and then he disappeared into it. The Bull arrived and butted the stone and broke it in two. Coyote jumped up quickly and ran away. He went along, and after a short distance he was out of breath again. Again he spoke, "I am already in danger." Somebody spoke to him, and he was told, "Come, come to me." That was a small bush and Coyote disappeared inside it. The Bull arrived and butted it, but missed it. He could not hit the little bush with his horns and get into it. Coyote said, "Stop, stop doing this to me! You cannot kill me." The Bull said to Coyote, "Now, come!" Then Coyote went near him.

Coyote said, "I'll fill my pipe, we will smoke." The Bull said, "It is well, let us smoke. What shall we smoke?" Coyote said, "Let us smoke block tobacco." The Bull said, "I don't smoke block tobacco." Coyote said, "What do you smoke?" "I smoke leaf tobacco." Coyote said, "It is well, let us smoke it. I have some." Then he filled his pipe and they smoked. Coyote said, "It will be this way in later times when there will be many people. When they are angry at one another, they will smoke to make their hearts feel good." The Bull said, "It is well. I'll tell you what happened to me. On this road, at the same place where my head lay, my wives were taken away from me. I had two wives and I came with them to this place. Then people came here, and I was killed." Coyote said, "Now you will be my friend. We shall get back your wives." Coyote looked at the horns of his friend. The points were broken off and he took his knife and sharpened them.

Coyote said to him, "Now let us go." Then the two friends went along. They saw tents, and Coyote said to his friend, "I'll stay here. Go get your wives and bring them back." Then the Bull went to get back his wives. He took them back, but the people made war on him. The Bull went back to where Coyote was staying. Coyote arose when he saw his friend coming. The Coyote attacked the people. There were four of them — two men and two women. The people saw that there were two of them now — the Bull and Coyote. They were afraid and they left. The friends went along and then stopped. The Bull spoke, and said to Coyote, "Look at my two wives! Which one do you want to take? She shall be your wife." Coyote looked at them and thought, "I think I will take the younger one." He said to Bull, "I take this one." They said to each other, "We will part now." They shook hands and said good-bye.

Coyote and his wife went off. Coyote saw a mountain in front and said to his wife, "That place looks like a valley. Go there and I shall go roundabout." The Buffalo Cow went on and Coyote went another way. He went quickly and got to the place where his wife was going. He sat down. After a short time the Cow arrived. Coyote thought, "I will shoot her and then I will eat her. I am hungry." As the Cow walked along, Coyote shot her and killed her. There she lay. A little ways off there was a flat stone. He sat down on the flat stone. He sat there and began to cry for his wife whom he had killed.

After a little while many wolves arrived and ate the Cow. Coyote tried to stand up, but he stuck to the stone. He tried to get up, but he couldn't get off so the wolves ate the Cow. They ate it all, nothing was left. Coyote was then able to get up. He arose and his tail came off. He went over to the Cow, and there were only bones left. He thought, "Well, I will break the bones." He piled the bones together, and he was about to break them and someone said, "Nephew, I do not allow you to break bones." Coyote looked, and there was Badger Woman who said, "I'll break the bones while you hold my tail." Then he held Badger Woman's tail. She said, "Don't hold on too tightly, you will badger my tail." Coyote obeyed. Badger Woman took the bladder and put the marrow into it. It was a big, round piece of marrow. Badger Woman said, "I shall eat that much." Coyote also said, "I'll eat much." The Badger Woman ran away quickly, carrying the marrow. Coyote pursued her, but Badger Woman was eating all the time. When she had finished, she threw back the bladder and said to Coyote, "I suppose you want that." Badger Woman went off. Coyote took the bladder and licked it. It was greasy.

Coyote was left standing there with the remains of broken bones. He thought, "I will pile them together and pound them to pieces." He sat down and began to pound. A voice said, "Nephew, I won't allow you to break bones." He saw two women, they were two birds. They said, "We will pound it. Meanwhile go and get something that you may use for a spoon. When you see that there is a fire, come back." So Coyote started. He took a root out of the ground, pounded and dried it, and then waited. Finally, he saw a large fire and went back, but when he got there, nothing was left. He looked up a tree, and there was one of the birds. The other one was on another tree. One carried the grease and the other one the chopped bone. Coyote had nothing to eat of the game he had killed.

The Giant

There was a town. One day two brothers went out hunting. As they were going along, the older one saw a bighorn sheep and shot it. He carried it down, but toward sunset he became hungry. He thought, "I'll make a fire and roast a piece of meat. When I have finished eating, I will cut up the meat and dry it." Then he threw a piece of the bighorn sheep meat into the fire. When it was cooked he ate it, but it was without taste. He thought, "I'll cut a piece of my own body and I'll roast it in the fire." Then he cut a piece off of himself and threw it into the fire. When it was done he ate it. It tasted good. He cut off another piece and threw it into the fire and ate it. After two days he had devoured himself entirely. Only his bones were left. The younger brother had gone on home, and the following morning he thought, "I'll go and look for my older brother." He went along to the place where they had been hunting. When he arrived, he heard a strange sound. He stood still and listened. He heard the sound from a hill in front of him and walked there. A little way off there was a fire. He went there and heard his older brother making that noise. The older brother was saying, "Oh, I love my brother and it will take me two days to eat him!" When the younger brother arrived there, the older brother saw him and ran after him and killed him.

Meanwhile, those at home said they ought to look for the brothers. The older one's wife took her son and started looking for them. As they went along, the woman heard a sound. She went in that direction and saw her husband sitting down. He was saying, "Oh, I love my son! It will take me two days to eat him." The woman was behind a hill and something told her, "Take sharp stones and stick them on your clothing. He will strike you and the stones will cut him. Then he will not be able to catch you." Then she stuck stones on her clothing and went nearer. He struck her, and he was cut. She carried her child, but her husband could not catch her. She started to run and he pursued her. Because he was only bones, he could not run fast.

When she got back, she said, "My husband ate his younger brother, and he intended to eat my son. He is coming." Then they said, "We will move camp." Someone said, "Who has enough courage to stay and kill him when he comes?" Coyote said, "I will stay," but everyone said, "Don't." Crane, said, "I will stay," and he was told, "That is good." Crane and the wife and the son of the older brother stayed. Everyone else moved from camp, but the three stayed there. Not long after Crane left too.

Then the brother arrived, but there was nobody left except his wife and his son. When he saw his wife, he said to her, "Give me the child." She gave it to him. When he took it, he killed it. He thought he would eat it, but his wife said to him, "Hand it to me, I shall go and wash it." He gave it to his wife and she carried it down to the water. Then she went behind and threw it away. She began to run after the other people. When she reached them, she said, "He arrived at the place where we moved camp. He has killed his boy." Then Crane was told, "Go back and kill him." Crane went back. He made a hole as long as his legs in a steep bank. Then he stayed there.

The brother remained at the camp. When his wife did not come back, he thought, "I'll go and kill her," so he went in the direction in which she had gone. There was nothing there. Only his son was lying there, and he ate him. Then he started in the direction in which his wife had gone. He went along the steep bank. The trail passed close to the bank, and Crane stayed there waiting. The brother did not know that Crane was there. He walked past that hole and when Crane saw him, he stretched out his foot quickly and kicked him over the bank. The brother fell into the water and was killed. Then Crane went off.

Coyote and the Ducks

Well, I'll tell you about Coyote and his children and what they did to the Ducks a long time ago.

21

Coyote was going along carrying his son and they came down to a lake named Where-They-Fight-With-Broken-Pieces-of-Wood-in-the-Lake. Coyote knew that far away there were many Ducks. He was hungry for them, but had no way of getting at them. He thought, "I'll fool the Ducks." He said to his son, "Go out and shout, 'Oh, my father's brothers-in-law!'" The child said what his father had told him and Coyote also cried, "Oh, my brothers-in-law! Oh, my brothers-in-law!" One Duck was swimming farther away on the water. He thought Coyote and his son were manitous and said to his children, "Wait, listen to what the manitous are saying!" There were many Ducks there and they listened to what the manitous were crying. Someone said, "Go ashore and ask him something." Then one of them went ashore. He said to Coyote, "Why do you say that?" Coyote said, "We wanted to play with you. You are playing nicely, but we are not able to go on the water." The Duck went back and said, "They want to play like we do." Then one of the Ducks said, "Go ashore. Take them and play with them." The Ducks went ashore and helped Coyote and his son so they would not sink, but they did not give them their feathers. Coyote and his son were told, "Now let us go together!" Then they went out together — Coyote, his son, and the Ducks. They played with the Ducks and while they were at play, all the Ducks flew along to another lake. They flew there, but Coyote went ashore overland. When he came to the water, he swam, but the Ducks flew again to the other lake. All at once Coyote laid down a rule. He said to them, "It is bad for you to fly away. Don't do it any more. Swim there through the middle of the water. Arrange yourselves in a line right across, and all of you dive together." The Ducks said to one another, "It is good, what the manitou says. Let us do it!" Then the Ducks did so.

At night Coyote went ashore and stretched a rope across the brook. Then the Ducks came diving along, and did not do anything. He caught the first one, the next one that came diving along he let go, and he caught the last one. He said to the other Ducks, "When you start diving, close your eyes. Don't look!" Coyote was clever. He thought they might see his trap. They did as he said for several days and Coyote ate many of them. The Ducks began to notice that there were fewer of them and they said among themselves, "We are getting few in number." One Duck said, "The wind is blowing from the place where Coyote's tent is and I smell burnt fat. Let us go and look into his tent." One Duck was called Great Diver. He dived and came to Coyote's tent. He went ashore and saw many dried ducks. Then he knew what Coyote had done. He went back, and when he came back he said, "It is Coyote. He is killing all of us. Then the Ducks cried and said among themselves, "He will do the same to us tomorrow. Look out when you dive! You will see whether there is anything in the stream." Then on the following day the Ducks started diving to another lake. The first ones all looked, and it was not long before they saw something right across the water. They dived and went back. Coyote said, "Oh, you are very smart! I was going to kill all of you." The Ducks did not dive any more, but flew away.

Lynx's tent was nearby. He went out. The wind was blowing his way and he smelled the burning fat. He followed the smell and arrived at the lake. He saw that Coyote and his son had much to eat, so he made them go to sleep. While Coyote and his son slept, Lynx took the Ducks. Then he took Coyote by his tail and pulled it. Coyote now had a long tail, and he also took Coyote's son and pulled his face so that he had a long face. Then he started back. Coyote's son woke up, and saw his father sleeping. He saw that he had a long face and a long tail. Then the son laughed at him because he was that way. He woke Coyote. Coyote looked at his son, and he saw that he was different from what he had been, and he looked at the Ducks, and they were gone. He said to his son, "I'll go after him." Coyote started out and saw a tent. He knew it was the tent of Lynx and his son and knew that Lynx had stolen the food. He made Lynx and his son sleep, and he took back the Ducks. Coyote took hold of Lynx's tail and pushed it in and he did the same to his son. Just a little piece of tail remained sticking out. He took Lynx's face and pushed it in, and he had a short face. Then he went back. Lynx and his son awoke. They saw how they were, and that there was no food. Therefore Coyote has a long nose and a long tail. Lynx did it. And therefore Lynx has a short nose and a short tail. Coyote did it.

Now I have told you about Coyote, and what he did to the Ducks long ago.

Origin of the Seasons

Well, I will tell you a story of what happened long ago in this world. Some people were staying at a certain place a long time ago, and summers and winters were long.

There was a town. It was winter time. A man named Coyote went into the tent of an old woman, who gave him food. The old woman was named Squirrel. Squirrel said, "There is no more food, and it will be a long time before spring will come. What shall I do? There is no more food." Coyote said, "Well, cry. Then if the people come in and ask you, 'Why do you cry?' don't answer. When they have all spoken to you, I shall say to you, 'Do you say that your food will be gone long before spring comes?' Then you say, 'Yes!' " Then Coyote went out.

Squirrel thought that what he had said was good. Then she cried and cried aloud. The people in the town said, "What is the old woman saying?" They went there and questioned her, but she did not speak. She kept on crying aloud. Then everyone questioned her, but the old woman did not speak. Coyote went there and said to the old woman, "Do you say that you will have no more food for a long time?" Then the old woman cried no more. She said, "Yes.!" The people said, "What shall we do to make spring come?"

There was another town, and this was where they kept the seasons. After twelve months had passed, these people would untie the springtime and the summertime and the fall of the year. Then they would tie up the winter. The people in the first town said, "What shall we do about the seasons? Let us go and steal the spring."

Then they started. They arrived at that town and said, "Whoever can walk secretly will go first." There was a boy who was known for his quiet walk. He was told, "You shall steal it." Then he started. He almost came to the tent and there he worked his manitou power. After he had done so, his manitou spoke to him, and told him what he was to do when he entered, and where spring was hanging. The boy took some gum and entered the tent. Meanwhile, the people said, "Whoever can throw farthest shall take the spring after it has been thrown out. Then he shall throw it away and the one who is strongest shall stay on the prairie on the hillside. It will be thrown there, and when he catches it, he shall open it at once." There was one very strong man. His manitou was Grizzly Bear. He was told, "You shall open it."

Meanwhile, the youth went in. He saw an old woman standing there. She said to him, "It is midwinter." Then he said to her, "Where is the springtime?" He was told, "It is hanging there." He said to her, "Where is the summer?" and she told him. He was holding the gum. He held it in his hand close to the fire. The woman thought that he was warming his hands, for it was cold. She did not know that he was heating the gum. After some time it melted. Then he grabbed the old woman, stuck the gum on her mouth, and went to get the thing in which she had said the springtime was kept. He pulled it off and carried it out. Then the old woman ran out quickly. She tried to speak, but could not because gum was stuck on her mouth. All her people could see was the old woman moving her arms and pointing in a certain direction. When her people got there, she pointed to her tent. They looked in, and the springtime was gone. They looked for it, and discovered that the people were carrying it away. Then they began to pursue the people. They wanted to kill all those who had stolen the spring. When they were about to overtake the people, the one who could throw farthest took the springtime and threw it. There on the prairie on the hill the strong one was standing. He worked his manitou power and turned into a Grizzly Bear. He caught the springtime because he was strong. The thing that contained it was strong, but he opened it. There was a wind and it was not long before there was no more snow, and it was spring. Now spring has six months, and there are six months in winter. The old woman did it when there was no food.

Now I have told you how the world was long ago.

Coyote Juggles With His Eyes

Well, I'll tell you what Coyote did with his eyes a long time ago. As Coyote went along, he saw a man running along and then stopping. Coyote went closer so he could watch. He saw the man running along and stopping again, and then looking up. Coyote went right up to the man, but the man did not see him. Coyote saw that the man stopped again and was taking out his eyes to throw them up. Then the man ran over and stood under the spot where the eyes were coming down, stopped and looked up, and his eyes came back down into his head.

Coyote thought, "Well, I'll take his eyes," and he went behind him. The man still did not see Coyote. He was busy throwing his eyes up again, but this time Coyote ran after them and caught the eyes. When the man looked up, his eyes did not come down again so he was without eyes. The one without eyes was named Snipe and now Snipe had no eyes. He went on, but Coyote was ahead of him and stretched out his fingers and just put them into Snipe's orbits. Snipe almost fell down. Then he went on, and Coyote did the same thing again. Snipe thought, "It is just as though somebody is doing this. If it should happen again, even it it hurts, I shall not mind it. I'll stretch my hands out." Coyote did so again. Even though it hurt him, Snipe stretched out his hands, felt that a man was there, and took hold of him. When Coyote knew that he was caught, he said, "Oh, don't do anything to me! I will give you your eyes." Snipe would not listen. Coyote was caught. His eyes were taken out, and Snipe put on Coyote's eyes. Then Snipe could see again and he knew Coyote had taken his eyes from him. So Snipe ran away, and Coyote was left with no eyes.

Snipe went back to his town and when he arrived he said, "I have Coyote's eyes here." Coyote tried to follow Snipe, but he couldn't see. He knew there were trees around and he thought gum would feel good. He felt for it, took it off, and put it into his eye sockets. He could see with it. Then Coyote had eyes again. He started after Snipe and saw the place where Snipe had gone. As he went along, the gum melted because of the heat, fell out, and Coyote was again without eyes. He tried to keep going, but couldn't see again. He knew there was a creek there. He thought, "The foam will feel good." He felt it, found it, stuck it on, and he had eyes again. He started walking along, but the foam was too soft. It burst, and Coyote was again without eyes. He went along and heard a child crying, "Sister, Sister!" He also heard someone else calling, "Here is a big berry patch." Coyote thought, "There must be huckleberries here." He felt with his hands for them and picked off a big one. He put it in his eyes and he had eyes again. He thought, "Now I have eyes again." He went to where the child was calling for his sister. The child thought that his sister was coming and so did not look. When Coyote arrived, he took hold of the child, took out his eyes, and so he had eyes again. Then Coyote went over where there were many huckleberries and cried, "Sister, here is a big berry patch." Then he sat down. The girl went there where her younger brother was sitting. She picked berries. Coyote arose, took hold of the girl and took out her eyes.

Then he went on to the town. There at one end was the tent of an old woman where he entered and ate. He said to her, "What are the pople doing in this town?" She said, "Coyote's eyes were brought here. They are using them to obtain good luck. After a little while my granddaughters will come. They will carry me to the dance." He asked her, "Do you dance?" The old woman said, "I am old. Only young men and women dance." Then he killed the old woman, took off her skin, and threw away her body. He went into her skin and sat down. After a short time her granddaughters came. When they arrived, they said, "Grandmother, we came to get you. They are dancing again so we will take you over there." Then they took Coyote on the back and carried him along. While he was being carried there, he said to the girls, "I will sing and I will dance."

When the two girls arrived, they said, "The old woman also wants to dance." Snipe said, "Well, she shall dance then." Then they danced. Coyote knew what to do. The old woman was told, "Now you sing!" Then, while the dancing was going on, they sang, "Try to get good luck out of Coyote's, Coyote's eyes!"

The old woman sang the same song, but she was not an old woman, she was Coyote. There was no light where they were dancing and the two girls were told, "Let the old woman stand up and lead her. She is old and weak." Then the two girls made their grandmother stand up and they danced. They tried hard, because the old woman was singing and this made them glad. They danced for a long time. Then the old woman said, "Let me carry the eyes." The girls were carrying the eyes of Coyote, so they gave them to her and they all danced about. Then it was noticed that the voice of the old woman was becoming fainter. She was almost out of breath, and it became hard to hear her. Then she was heard singing by the doorway. Then she was not heard anymore. They stopped, and did not dance anymore. They said, "Bring a light. Look for the old woman! She may have died of fatigue." They brought a light and they looked for the old woman. Then they saw the skin lying there. The old woman was gone and only her skin remained. They heard Coyote some distance away. He laughed, and they said, "It was Coyote. It was not the old woman who danced. Coyote killed her. It was only her skin."

Now I have told you what Coyote did to his eyes.

Wolf

Well, now I will tell you what Wolf did long ago.

There was a town, and a man was named Wolf. He was married to a woman in another camp whose name was Doe. When his wife made moccasins for him, they were bad, but when she made moccasins for her elder brothers, they were good. This angered Wolf and he left his wife. He went back to his own town. When he arrived, he said, "Let us start for my wife's town and fight the people there!" Then they started, but before they arrived, the Wolf's brother-in-law knew they were coming because he had spirit power. He also knew that they were angry with him. The brother-in-law, who was a two-year-old Buck, sang to his spirit. Then he said to his wife, "The Wolves are mad at us." He dug a hole, and let his wife and his son go in. Then the many warriors arrived where Buck was singing, but because of his spirit power, he had become a deer and became what his name was. He went up to the top of a mountain. Wolf killed all the people and looked for his brother-in-law, but he did not see him. Wolf knew that Buck had spirit power and he thought, "I shall not be able to kill him."

Then Wolf went to his home and sang and he became a wolf. He looked and because he was working his spirit power, he saw the tracks of the brother-in-law. He followed the tracks and saw him on top of a mountain. His brother-in-law was standing there, facing this way. Wolf started up, but the one who had become a young Buck saw him. By the time Wolf arrived Buck was gone, and there was another high mountain. Wolf went down and went up toward the top and found his tracks. He came to another high mountain and saw Buck standing on top. Again Wolf went up. Buck saw the Wolf starting, and went down to a river. Buck thought, "I'll go to my father's father, Fish." Fish's tent was on the other side of the river. When Wolf stepped down to the place where his brother-in-law had been standing, he was not there, but Wolf saw his tracks going down. He followed them thinking, "Fish is bad. Maybe he will not give Buck to me. If I do not catch him, and if he enters Fish's tent, I shall not be able to get him."

Meanwhile, Buck arrived at Fish's tent and went in. Fish was sitting inside. Buck told Fish, "Put me somewhere, Wolf is pursuing me." Fish did not look at him. Buck spoke again, but again Fish did not look at him. He just sat there and smoked. Buck said again, "Hurry up! Wolf has almost arrived. He'll kill me." Fish said, "Is he a wolf?" Buck said, "Yes, he has become a wolf." Fish said, "Can you transform yourself into a deer?" Buck said, "He is just outside. I became a man when I came in." Fish said, "Lie down there!" Buck laid down. Fish touched his deerskin mittens, threw them on Buck, and said, "Don't move!" Buck thought, "I thought he would do something for me, that's why I came in." There was just one mitten which Fish threw on him. Buck was big, and his legs stuck out. Then he saw Wolf come in.

Buck thought he would be seen by Wolf. He did not turn his eyes from Wolf, but Wolf did not see him. Now Wolf retransformed himself into a man. When he was about to enter the tent of Fish, he said to him, "Didn't you see Buck?" Fish did not look at him, but did the same as he had done with Buck. Wolf kept asking him the same question. After a while Fish spoke and said to him, "Your talk is bad. He is your brother-in-law. You should love each other. Why are you angry at him?" Then he asked, "Did Buck transform himself into a deer?" Wolf said, "Yes, he transformed himself." Fish said, "Why should he come into my tent if he is a deer? If he should come into my tent, he would become a man. Go out and look for him. Maybe he went into the water. Game sometimes does that." Then Wolf went out. As soon as he left, Fish made a figure of grass and hurriedly threw it out of the smoke hole. The figure became a deer, which stood there on the other side of the water. When Wolf went out, he saw Buck standing in the water on the other side. Wolf went in again, and said to Fish, "Give me a canoe. I see a deer on the other side." Fish said, "You said you became a wolf and Buck became a deer. Later on, when a wolf runs after a deer and it goes into the water of a river, then the wolf also will swim across." Wolf said, "Is that so?" and went out.

Wolf transformed himself into a wolf and then he swam across. Fish had told a lie. It was not a deer standing in the water, it was grass that he had made into a deer. Once Wolf was gone, Buck arose and said to Fish, "Take me across, so that I may kill him, for he killed all my relatives." Then Fish arose, took his blanket, and put it on Buck. He took his belt, his hat, and his mittens. Buck said, "Hurry up! He is about to swim across." Fish said, "He is still here." Then he went out and launched his canoe. He did not hurry, and Wolf had almost gotten across. Then Fish and Buck went aboard. Fish took his paddle, put it into the water, and pushed with it. He almost caught up with Wolf. Then he put the paddle in on the other side, and caught up with Wolf. As Buck was about to shoot Wolf, who did not see him, he touched his canoe, and it made a little noise. Wolf heard the canoe, looked at it, and Buck was standing in the water, about to shoot him. Wolf said to him, "Oh brother-in-law! I love you, don't kill me!" Buck said, "I shall not take pity on you because you have killed all my relatives." Wolf was shot and killed. Fish said, "Go back to your wife. Your son is poor."

Now I have told all that happened in olden times.

Skunk

Well, I'll tell you what the brothers Skunk and Fisher did long ago.

Skunk and his brother Fisher lived in a tent. Nearby was the tent of Frog and her granddaughters, Chipmunk and Big Chipmunk. Chipmunk was hungry for meat, and began to complain. Her grandmother said to her, "Oh granddaughter, granddaughter! What do you mean?" Chipmunk said, "I am hungry." Her grandmother said to her, "Take whatever you hunger for." Chipmunk said, "I am hungry for meat." Her grandmother said to her, "Take a little piece of dried meat. Eat it," but Chipmunk did not take it. She was asked, "Do you want fresh meat?" and she replied, "Yes." Then her grandmother, Frog, said to her, "Go to Fisher. He shall be your husband, but don't look at Skunk. He is bad. Only Fisher shall be your husband. Fisher is never hungry because he is a skillful hunter."

Then the sisters Chipmunk and Big Chipmunk started to go and see Fisher. Their grandmother said to them, "When you get there, stay at a distance. After a while, in the evening you will see Fisher coming back. Then you may go near." When the sisters arrived at the tent, they stayed at a distance, but Skunk knew already that the two girls were coming because he had spirit power. He also knew the moment they arrived. Skunk

31

was always pounding bones. He worked his spirit power, took Fisher's blanket, put it on, and went out. Then his spirit pounded bones for him. Chipmunk said, "Let us go near! There is Fisher. He is at home." She was told by her older sister, "That is not Fisher who came out, it is Skunk." Chipmunk said, "How could that be? I can hear the noise of Skunk pounding bones inside." She was told by her older sister, "It is not Skunk who makes the noise. Skunk's spirit does it." Chipmunk kept insisting and finally her older sister said, "Well, let us go, but do not feel badly about it if it is not Fisher. You urge me to go. Our grandmother said to wait until evening before we go there." So they started and when they arrived, they saw Skunk alone there. Skunk gave them meat which they ate. Then he said, "Your grandmother wants me to marry you." Skunk prepared a place in the rear of the tent and said to them, "Stay here." Then the sisters went to the rear of the tent and stayed there. Skunk was pounding dried meat all the time.

Then Fisher came home. He said to Skunk, "Go and get some water, I want to drink." He threw his drinking horn to him. Fisher's water was far away and Skunk thought, "Fisher might find the girls." He arose, took dried meat and threw it backward to the sisters saying, "Divide-de-de-de it." On his way out he sang, "Don't move-hoo-hoo-hoov." Then Skunk started, but he thought, "Fisher's water is far away. I shall go to my water." He arrived there quickly and dipped it up. Then Skunk started to run back. He thought, "I want to get back quickly. He might go off with those girls." He came back and gave the water to his younger brother. Fisher took it, and knew that it was Skunk's water, so threw it down and said, "This is not my water. It is your water." Skunk went out again, but dipped up the water quickly and came right back. He came back so quickly that he spilled it while running. Now there are many little lakes, the result of what Skunk spilled while running. Then he came home and gave water to his brother.

After Fisher had drunk, he said to Skunk, "Go and get my game." Fisher had known while he was away that the two girls had arrived to see him and not Skunk. For this reason, he was angry with his older brother. Fisher took entrails and painted them red. When Skunk was told to bring in the meat, Fisher gave him the painted entrails and told him, "Go quickly, because the sun is getting low." Then Skunk was really afraid that Fisher might go off with the two girls. Again he took dried meat and threw it backward and said, "Divide-de-de-de it. Don't move-hoo-hoo-hoov!" Then Skunk started out and came to the place where the meat was. He tied it with that line, but he did not know that the line was entrails. He thought it was a line because it was painted red. When he put it on his back and arose, the line broke. Then Skunk said, "Oh, I broke my brother's tump line!" It began to grow dark and cold.

After Skunk had gone, Fisher said to the girls, "Now come out! Why did you come here so early? You ought to have come later on. Now eat some meat! After you have eaten, we will move away." Then the sisters ate meat. After they had eaten, Fisher told them, "Now we will move! Skunk is bad. He has spirit power and will kill us all. There in the corner of the tent are all his rotten bones. Take them all out." Then the sisters took out Skunk's bones. Fisher then said, "Where shall we go? Skunk knows where my tent is." Chipmunk said, "Let us go to my tent!" They went to Chipmunk's tent, but Fisher could not go in, for it was too small. Then Big Chipmunk said, "Let us go to my tent!" When they arrived, they went in, but Fisher could not go in. Fisher said, "Then let us go to my tent, although Skunk knows where it is!" Then Fisher worked his spirit power, and two trees stood there. He transformed himself, and became a real fisher. He transformed his other wife, and she became a real chipmunk. Then they climbed one of the trees and stayed there.

Fisher had caused a windstorm. It was very cold and Skunk thought Fisher would cause him to freeze to death. He left the tump line at the door. He still did not know that it was entrails. He thought, "I'll leave this meat." Then, when it was dark, he left it and went out. When he got back, he knew that they had moved camp. There was no fire so he cried. He thought, "I'll die, because it is so cold." Skunk said, "Chief, chief!" and looked for his rotten bones, but they were all gone. Then he found one rotten bone in a hole. He went in and was glad. He thought, "Now I am saved." He stayed there that night. Early in

33

the morning he was heard talking. Fisher asked the sisters, "Big Chipmunk, did you take out all his rotten bones?" Big Chipmunk said, "I took them all." Chipmunk said, "There is one bone that I did not take." Fisher said, "Then Skunk will kill us all. He is bad and that rotten bone is his spirit power. Now he cannot die. He will make war on us."

Skunk came out and sang. He worked his spirit power and became a real skunk. Long ago the skunk was large. He killed everything, even strong animals. When he became a real skunk he sang and said, "Burnt rocks, burnt rocks, remains of burnt bone!" He finished singing and said, "There is a faint sound on the other side." Then he sprayed the tree with his musk, and the tree was no longer standing there. Then he sent his musk to the other side, and that tree was no longer standing there. There were only two trees left and he sprayed his musk to one of them. Fisher and his wives came out quickly and jumped across to the other tree. He sent his musk to the other side, and they jumped across to the other tree. Skunk kept spraying his musk and finally Chipmunk grew tired and fell down. Skunk went to Chipmunk and sent his musk into her mouth and she died. Then he shot his musk at Fisher's other wife and Big Chipmunk also fell down and she was killed. Then only Fisher remained. After some time, Skunk sprayed his musk again. Then Fisher became tired and also fell down. Skunk killed Fisher's wives and Fisher. Skunk stayed there. He took the sisters and he restored them to life. Then they became his wives.

Skunk said, "Where shall we go now? Fisher is bad. If he should come to life he will kill us all." Big Chipmunk said, "Let us go to my tent!" When Skunk had killed them all, be became a man again, and the sisters became women. Then Big Chipmunk started for her tent. They entered, but it was too small. Skunk said, "Come out!" Big Chipmunk came out. Skunk used his spirit power to make the tent larger. They entered and went to bed. Skunk lay in the middle, and his wives did not sleep. He said to them, "Let us sleep! I am tired." They did not listen to him, but they tickled him. They did this so that he should not sleep. Then Skunk became very sleepy and said to them, "It's enough, let us play later on." Still they tickled him again, and finally Skunk slept. Even though they tickled him, he did not wake up. When the sisters saw that Skunk was really dead asleep, they said to each other, "Now let us go to Fisher!" They arose and moved Skunk. The tent was on a mountain, and they turned Skunk so that his head was toward the door, and his legs lay toward the mountains. The the sisters went out again and sang. They worked their spirit power, and the size of Big Chipmunk's hole was almost the size of Skunk. The stones squeezed him all over. Then Big Chipmunk and her sister went back to where Fisher lay.

When they got there, they restored him to life and when Fisher arose, he saw his wives. He said to them, "Where is Skunk?" They said to him, "He is in a hole in the mountain." He said to them, "Let us go to a faraway country. Skunk is bad. No matter how strong the stones, he will break them and will come out again." Then Fisher and his wives started and left the country.

Skunk was asleep, but he began to wake up and knew that his wives hurt him. He said, "Move away a little! You hurt me!" They did not move and he said again, "Move away a little!" He pushed them and then noticed that what he touched was hard. Then he moved, and everything was tight against his body. He was in a hole in the rock. It was all around him on each side of his body and on top of his body. He could not move so he cried. He thought, "I will die." He knew that he used to break rocks, so he began to spray the rocks with his musk. After awhile he could move his leg. Then the space got large, but he could not see the daylight yet. He thought, "Let me lie the other way," and he turned the other way. After awhile his power caused the rocks to split. After sometime he saw a little hole. Then the rocks opened and he said, "Oh, it looks like a star!" The hole grew larger and he thought, "Now let me see how large the hole is." He took out his musk bag and put it on the end of his bow and stuck it out.

Raven was going along at this time and saw what Skunk was doing. He stood there outside and when Skunk put out his musk bag, he passed it in front of Raven. Raven did not look at it and after some time Skunk took his musk bag in again. He smelled of it and said, "I think it smells like the eye of Raven.

Maybe he is coming this way. He is one who is always going about." Raven had not looked at it because he knew that Skunk would smell it. Skunk put it out again and sang his spirit song.

Raven transformed himself into a raven, and took hold of Skunk's musk bag with his bill. Then he flew away, because he had become a real raven who could fly. Skunk heard the flapping of wings and said, "Oh!" He pulled in his bow quickly, but his musk bag was gone. Then he cried and said, "Chief, Chief!" for his power had been taken away from him. He said to himself, "You always make too much noise about your own ears. Now, listen instead of crying." Then Skunk listened. He noticed that Raven went right up, then came down making a noise. Then the noise stopped. Skunk was left lying there so he took his knife and cut off his leg and pushed it out. Because the hole was small, he could not get out all at once. He also cut off the other leg and pushed it out. He cut off his arm and put it out, too. Now there was one arm left. He cut it off, and it rolled out. Then all his limbs were gone. He sang,

"Let my back roll out,
Let my back roll out."

Then his back rolled out. Then he rolled out. He rolled himself on one arm. He took the other one and stuck it on. He took his legs and he stuck on both of them. Then Skunk arose and stood up, but something was wrong. He had no belly. Then he went and took leaves and put them in. Then he was almost whole again.

He started after Raven who had flown across the mountains. Skunk went across the mountains, and he came to the prairie. After a long time he came to a town. When Raven had arrived, he had transformed himself into a man, and told everyone, "I have brought Skunk's musk bag with me." Then everyone was glad and said, "Now Skunk will no longer kill everything. He has no musk bag." Then they played with it for a long time. Then Skunk came. He had become a man again. They saw a man coming along, and asked him, "Who are you?" Skunk answered, "I come from that prairie over there. I am called Coming- from- the- Prairie- Far- Away- with- Head- Washed-with-White-Clay-Carrying-My-Bow-Sideways." They said,

"The tent of the chief, Raven, is over there. He just came to this town and brought Skunk's musk bag with him."

There were two chiefs in this town, Raven and Grizzly Bear. Skunk went to Raven's tent and Raven brought out the musk bag. Raven worked over it, and it became a pup. Skunk did not go into the tent, but stopped at the doorway where the pup was tied. It went to him gladly and said, "What did they do to me, Skunk?" It knew him, but Raven did not know that it was he. Then Skunk sat down and was given food. The food didn't help him because there was nothing in him. He was dry inside and so did not eat much. Grizzly Bear said to Skunk, "You should go out," so Skunk arose and went out. Where he had been sitting, was a pile of meat. A child said, "There is some meat." Raven said, "Don't eat it. He dropped it from his mouth, so children must not eat it. I'll eat it myself." Meanwhile, Skunk entered Grizzly Bear's tent and was given food. Here again he could not eat much. When he went out, he left meat behind again and Grizzly Bear himself ate it. Because Skunk had no belly, the meat went right through him.

Then, when it was almost evening, Raven went out, saying, "Come out and play! You have a toy." Then they all went out. They brought the pup and put it down a short distance away. They kicked it. It ran, and they ran after it. When they caught up with it, they kicked it. Then Skunk had pity on his musk bag. When it saw him, it almost ran up to him, but he nodded his head the other way. Skunk thought, "I am thirsty and it might hurt me. Later on, tomorrow, I'll take it back." At night they stopped playing. Then Skunk went to the river, jumped in and soaked himself. All day long he soaked himself. When the sun was going down, they played again and Skunk thought, "I'll take back my musk bag." They went on playing, but Skunk sat down a little way off. He thought, "It might hurt me." They chased it toward him, and it went there. Then it turned around and it came back. Skunk nodded his head to it, and it came running his way. It came, and they could not catch up with it. Then Skunk turned himself toward it, and his musk bag went to him. It got into him again and threw him down. Skunk got up. They said to one another, "Don't look at him, for it is

Skunk. He himself took back his musk bag." Their toy was gone.

Now I have told what Skunk and his brother did.

Frog and Antelope

Well, I'll tell you how Frog won over Antelope a long time ago.

There was a town named Fish Hawk Nest. Antelope was the chief of the town. Antelope was a fast runner, even the best runners were beaten by him. He had spirit power and won over everybody.

There was another town called Frogs. The chief Frog thought, "I'll cheat Antelope." He said to his tribe, "Let us play with Antelope!" They said to him, "What shall we do with Antelope? He runs fast." He said to them, "We shall go, all of us and we shall play with him." Then he told his people what to do. All the Frogs said, "Well, your thoughts are good." The chief said, "I'll go alone. If Antelope agrees, tomorrow we will all go." The Frogs said, "It is well."

Then the chief Frog started. When he arrived at Antelope's tent, Antelope said to him, "Why do you come to my tent?" Frog said, "I come here to see if you are not afraid to run a race with me." Antelope laughed. He thought, "Even if he runs fast, I can easily beat Frog." Antelope said, "If you win, my property shall be your property. If I win, you may give your property to me." Frog said, "I agree and I'll take your property." Then everyone in town laughed at him because he would not beat Antelope. Frog said, "Tomorrow just at noon I'll come, accompanied by my tribe." Then Frog left.

When he returned home, he said to his tribe, "Now we will cheat Antelope and his children." On the following morning the Frogs all went to Fish Hawk Nest. There were many Frogs. Even the women went along with the men Frogs. When they were almost at the town, the chief Frog said, "Before anyone comes out, go and lie down on the trail where the race will be. Lie so far apart and each of you take a turn running." Then the Frogs went to the starting place, and all of them laid down where it was their spot to run. They laid down up to the point where the track turned. When this was done, the other Frogs went to town to announce their arrival. Then Antelope and his children went to the starting place. The Frogs bet their property, and the Antelopes bet their clothes. They staked much because they thought the Frogs would be beaten. They thought they would win.

When the race was about to start, Antelope stood up. He laughed at his enemy. Frog was lying there and he just looked at Antelope. They said, "Now, start!" Frog jumped, but Antelope laughed. His enemy looked funny to him. Antelope did not run fast when Frog gave his first jump. Then another Frog that was lying there jumped up, and all the Frogs did the same. Antelope did not go very fast and soon was left behind. Then Antelope ran more quickly. He was still left far behind. He ran fast, but even when he ran fast, the Frogs were ahead of him. Then he arrived at the turning place, and when he got there, the Frogs laid down in the opposite direction. Then Antelope turned back, but the Frogs were always ahead of him. Antelope tried hard, but he knew that he would be beaten. Antelope was not even near the starting point when Frog arrived. They all laughed, but Antelope's people were sick at heart because Frog had won. Frog wasn't out of breath, but Antelope was puffing. He lay on his back and said, "You beat me, Frog." Then Frog took what he had won. He went back and those who laid down on the track didn't move. In the evening they got up and went back, and it was heard by all that Frog had beaten Antelope.

Now I have told you how Frog beat Antelope in olden times.

Kalispel Myths

Coyote, Wren, and Grouse

Once Coyote met Wren and laughed at his small bow and arrows. He said, "You can't shoot far with those." Wren answered, "Yes, I can shoot far. If you go to that distant ridge I will shoot you while you are there." Coyote laughed and said, "That ridge is so far away that we can hardly see it." Soon afterward Coyote was walking along this ridge and Fox was following him. He had forgotten about his talk with Wren. Presently he heard something coming and Wren's arrow struck him in the heart. He gave two jumps and fell down dead. Fox pulled out the arrow and jumped over Coyote, who came to life and said, "I must have slept a long time." Fox said, "You were not sleeping, you were dead. Wren's arrow struck your heart. Why do you fool with Wren? You know he can shoot better than anyone." Coyote took the arrow from Fox and said, "I shall get even with him."

Sometime after this, Coyote met Wren and proposed to gamble with him. Coyote said, "I have an arrow which looks like yours. Now you have a chance to win it back." They played a game of throwing arrows. Coyote beat Wren every time and won all his arrows. Then he won his bow, and later all his beautiful clothes. Wren was left practically naked. Coyote went off singing, "I won from the Kalispel." Wren followed him at some distance.

Coyote passed by the lodge of Willow-Grouse who had ten young children. Their parents were off in the hills. Coyote asked the children, "Who is your father?" They answered, "Flying-Past-Head." Coyote laughed and said, "No that cannot be his name." He asked the name of their mother, and they answered "Flying-Past-Between-the-Legs." He laughed saying, "No, that cannot be her name." He went into the lodge and dug a small hole near the fire. Then he said to the children, "Carry those red bearberries into the hole and watch me cook them for you." They did so and crowded around the edge to watch him. He pushed them into the hole and threw earth and hot ashes on top of them. When they were cooked, he went on.

The Grouse parents came home and cried when they found their children were dead. Wren came along and asked them why they cried and they told him. Wren said, "I have a grudge against Coyote, too. I want my things which he won from me. If you can get them back for me, I will restore your children to life." Coyote was then passing over a high ridge close to a steep cliff. The Grouse parents made a detour and hid ahead of him on the upper side. When Coyote was opposite them, one flew out suddenly at his head, and Coyote bent back over the cliff to avoid it. Then the other flew between his legs and Coyote lost his balance and fell over the cliff. While Coyote was falling, the Grouse parents took away his bow and arrows, quiver, and clothes. They gave these back to Wren, who then revived the Grouse children. Coyote was killed by the fall, but Fox found him and brought him back to life by jumping over him.

Coyote and the Snake-Monster

There was a huge rattlesnake-monster which occupied the Jocko Valley. Its tail was at a place near Evero and its mouth at Skullo near Ravalli. Its stomach was near Jocko. It swallowed people without their knowing it. They walked into its mouth and passed on to its stomach thinking they were going through a valley, and did not know that they were inside a monster. When they reached the stomach, they became sick and before long they died.

Coyote was travelling with Fox and reached that district. The people told him of the monster, and he said he would go and kill it. Coyote's cousin Fox, who was his travelling companion, advised him not to go because he would be killed. Coyote started anyway and when near the monster's head cut two long tamarack poles and carried them along on his shoulder. He thought, "I will use these in case he tries to close his mouth on me."

Coyote passed through the monster's mouth without knowing it. When he reached a place near Arlee, he saw a number of people in all stages of dying. He asked them what they were doing there and they answered, "The monster has killed us." He said, "Where is he? I am looking for him. I don't see anything here to kill you." Then they answered, "You have been swallowed. You are in its stomach now."

Then Coyote placed his poles upright and two tamaracks grow at this place today. Not very far from there he saw the monster's heart hanging down. Coyote was wearing a sharp arrow-stone fastened upright on his head. He began to dance and whenever he jumped up the stone pierced the heart. He kept on dancing in this way until he had killed the monster. Its heart may still be seen in the shape of a butte near Jocko. Coyote supported its mouth so that it could not close, and opened its tail. The cut he made may be seen as a canyon near Evero. Thus Coyote made it possible for people to pass through without hindrance or harm. When he finished, the valley was as we see it today.

Coyote and Mountain-Sheep

Coyote was travelling and came to Amtkane about five miles below Missoula, where a large rock is standing on the edge of a high cliff. It moves when it is pushed. Here lived the Mountain-Ram named Bighorn, who killed people. He invited passers-by to push the rock over the cliff. When they failed he invited them to look over the cliff at the sheep on the rocks below. Then while they were looking, he would push them over and kill them.

As Coyote was passing, Bighorn shouted to him. Coyote went up and asked him what he wanted. He saw that Coyote was armed so he said, "You have a bow and arrows. I should like you to shoot those sheep among the rocks below." Coyote went to look at them. Then Bighorn pushed him over and Coyote was killed on the rocks below. Later Fox came along

45

and jumped over him. Then Coyote moved, rubbed his eyes, and said, "I must have slept a long time." Fox answered, "You were dead. I told you not to come here." Coyote said, "I will be revenged."

Coyote went the same way and as he was passing, Bighorn shouted as before. Coyote asked him what he wanted. Bighorn said to him, "You have a bow and arrows. I want you to shoot these sheep." Coyote went cautiously to the edge of the cliff and pretended not to see the sheep. Bighorn pointed them out, but Coyote said he did not see them. Bighorn leaned out over the cliff to show them to Coyote, and Coyote shoved him over and killed him. Coyote said, "Had you kept on living and doing this way, you would have exterminated the people."

Coyote and the Shellfish Women

Coyote was travelling and went up the Bitter-Root river. There he saw a number of women dancing among tall grass on the bank. He crossed a ridge while approaching them and heard them singing, "He goes up the ridge." He said, "They have noticed me. They mean me." When he went down over the ridge they sang, "He goes down the ridge." Coyote thought, "They refer to me." He went down and joined the women. They took him by each hand and danced with him toward the river. They said, "We are going into the water." Coyote said, "Let me go. My clothes will get wet. I will take them off." They answered, "You need not mind. It does not matter about clothes in the other world where you are going." They took him into the water and dragged him up and down until he was drowned. They left his body on the bank and Fox came along and brought him to life by jumping over him. Coyote said, "I shall get even with these women."

He went back and found them dancing in the same place. He set fire to the grass all around them and they ran together to get away from the fire. When they saw that it would reach them, they rushed through and ran for the river. As they passed through the fire, they were scorched. Coyote transformed them saying, "You shall be shellfish and people shall put you into the fire and eat you." For this reason these shellfish appear as if burned on one side.

Coyote and Elk

Coyote went to Few-Trees-Standing-on-Prairie, a place near Hamilton on the Bitter-Root river, where an Elk-Monster lived. The monster lay on a butte where from which it could see a long distance over the adjoining prairie. Nothing could pass over the prairie without being seen by it. When it saw people it drew in its breath and they were sucked into its mouth and swallowed. It had thus killed many people.

Coyote took his wife, the Short-Tailed-Mouse, with him and ordered her to dig an underground passage to the Elk. She began to work behind a hill and tunnelled up to the Elk. Then her husband told her to move camp across the prairie. Coyote went through the passage and came out right under the Elk-Monster. The latter was surprised and said, "How did you come here? I never saw you, and I see everything." Coyote answered, "I came right across the prairie. You must be blind if you did not see me."

Elk became afraid because he thought Coyote must have greater powers than he had. Just then Coyote saw the people crossing the prairie. He asked Elk if he saw them and he answered, "Yes." Coyote said, "Then go and attack them. In the world whence I come we do that. When we see strangers, we go out to attack them and try to take their scalps." Elk agreed and Coyote accompanied him. Elk had a large stone dagger. Coyote said, "That knife will make you tired. It is too large and heavy for you to carry. Let me carry it for you." Elk gave him the knife, and thus disarmed himself. Then Coyote attacked him, stabbed him to death, and cut out his heart. He said, "Henceforth you shall be a common elk and people shall eat you, instead of your eating people."

47

The Wren

The Earth people wanted to make war on the Sky people. Grizzly Bear was the chief of the Earth people, and he called all the warriors together. They were told to shoot in turn at the moon (or sky). All did as directed, but their arrows fell short. Only Wren had not shot his arrow. Coyote said, "He need not shoot. He is too small, and his bow and arrows are too weak." However, Grizzly Bear declared that Wren must have his turn.

Wren shot his arrow and it hit the moon (or sky) and stuck fast. Then the others shot their arrows, each of which stuck in the neck of the preceding one until they had made a chain reaching from the sky to the ground. Then all the people climbed up, Grizzly Bear going last. He was very heavy and when he had climbed more than half way, his weight broke the chain. However, he made a spring and caught the part of the chain above him and this caused the arrows to pull out at the top where the leading warriors had made a hole to enter the sky. The whole chain fell down and left the people without a means of descending.

The Earth people attacked the Sky people (i.e., the Stars) and defeated them in the first battle, but the latter soon gathered in such numbers that they far outnumbered the Earth people, and in the next battle they killed a great number and routed them. The defeated Earth people ran for the ladder, but many were overtaken and killed on the way. When they found the ladder broken, each prepared himself the best way he could so as not to fall too heavily, and one after another jumped down. Flying Squirrel was wearing a small robe, which he spread out like wings when he jumped. Therefore, he has something like wings now. He came down without hurting himself. Whitefish looked down the hole before jumping, but puckered up his mouth and drew back when he saw the great depth. Therefore, he has a small puckered mouth to the present day. Sucker jumped down without first preparing himself and his bones were broken, and that is why the sucker's bones are found in all parts of its flesh now.

Coyote and His Son-in-Law

Coyote lived with his family. His wife was a wolf. While she was gathering wood, she caught a deer and shouted back to Coyote, "Come and kill it, I am holding the deer." He said, "Yes, but wait till I get some work done and some arrows fixed." She said, "Hurry," and he said, "When I get a box fixed." She said, "Hurry," and he said, "Wait till I get some twigs ready for snow-shoes." "Hurry, my arms are already stiff." He said, "Wait till I get them tied to my feet." Coyote finished and went. The wife was still holding the deer. There was a tree not far away. Coyote made a road up to the tree and said to his wife, "Well, get it on the road I have built, then let it go. When it comes running on the road in my direction, I'll shoot it." The woman got it there and let it go, but the deer started running in the other direction. Coyote said to his wife, "I'll follow the track, and when you come here on my track, come after me on the road. Wherever I kill it, I'll make a fire." Then Coyote was on his way chasing the deer.

Coyote had two children. The wolf was a girl, and the coyote was a boy. The wife packed them and walked along with the little children on her back. Coyote came out of the woods, just as the deer came out on a little open field. The deer went into the woods again. Not very far from there he came out on another little open field. The deer was quite close and Coyote was right behind him now. He ran after it and came very close, but his snow-shoes got heavy.

As the deer came out of the woods, it said to the mice, "Do something for me and I'll pay you with my hair, which your children can use for warming themselves." The mice were in the holes of Coyote's snow-shoes. Then he hit his snow-shoes, took some steps further and they got heavy again. He looked at them, and saw that wherever he hit his snow-shoes, there were lots of mice. He took off his blanket and put it on the ground. He took the mice, threw them all on the blanket, packed it, and walked to a place where he could find some wood. Then he made a fire. Coyote took the blanket and shook off some of the mice, saying, "These are for me." He took some more and shook them off, "These are for my wife." He shook off some more, "These are for my daughter." He took some more and shook them off, "These are for my son."

Then his wife came out of the woods into the little open field and saw the fire. She said to her children, "He must have killed the deer." She was watching as he took a mouse and threw it on the fire. When he had thrown it on the fire, he ran upon it again, took it, rubbed it in her hand, threw it in his mouth, and then chewed. He looked back at his wife and said to her, "Well, we thought too much of ourselves. This shall be your food, and this our daughter's food, and this our son's food." His wife said to him, "I don't think I'll eat it." She took the little boy and gave him to Coyote. Then she left Coyote. The boy was going to cry, but Coyote said to him, "Stop crying, we have got plenty of food." Then they ate it all up.

Then Coyote picked up his son and walked until they came down to the water. There were swans in the water and Coyote wept when he saw them. They said to him, "Why are you crying?" He said, "I pity the way you get your food. Haven't you got to be in straight lines when you are looking for food? Aren't your parents in straight lines? That's why I cry." He said to them, "It is for your parents that I cry, oohoohoohooh! There is a little creek a short way from here. Now, when you line up, you shall go upstream in that direction." They all went upstream. "Now you stay in a straight line, nobody lag behind. No, no, some of you are lagging behind." Then he said to the swans, "Why are some lagging behind?" They all lined up again. A short distance from there, there was a log lying across the creek. They came to the narrow passage where the log was lying. Coyote said, "You shall all go under it in the same way." They went under. He was watching as their heads went under, pushed on the log and crushed them. "Hahahahaha," Coyote laughed. He raised the log and put many swans on the bank.

Coyote said to his son — his son's name was Caucinsen, He-Washes-His-Ankle — "Here we'll build our house." Then he put up a house. They finished it and finally they fetched the swans, brought them in, and smoked them. Then Coyote and his son ate and afterward they went to sleep. The next morning he said to Caucinsen, "Wake up, you shall eat again." Caucinsen looked around and there was nothing left, everything was gone. He said to his father, "Oh, who has robbed us?" Coyote got up and looked around, but there was nothing left, it was really all gone. They starved, but they finally slept when night came. As Coyote fell asleep, he saw the thief and thought, "I am being robbed by the Lynx." When Coyote and his son were sleeping, Lynx had seen that Coyote had plenty of food. Coyote said to his son, "Wake up, Caucinsen, it is the Lynx who is robbing us." Then Caucinsen and his father went and stole lots from Lynx and carried it back. As Coyote and his son came back to their house, Coyote said to him, "I'll look around for my wife. You certainly have plenty of food now."

Then Coyote walked and looked for his wife. Then he saw a camp with many people and said to them, "Where is your chief?" He was told, "He lives over there in the big house." He went into the house and saw that the women were very beautiful. He was going to go away, but someone said to him, "I am here, your wife." He had planned to sit down at his daughter's side, but he said, "I am longing for my wife now." He did not know that these were his wife and his daughter. Finally he sat down. They took off his clothes and dressed him like a chief.

In the evening, the people gathered. Coyote's wife and daughter said to him, "Don't behave foolishly. When they come in, you withdraw a little." Then Coyote thought, "Why should I keep quiet, I am really too nicely dressed to sit still." A young man who was Coyote's son-in-law came in and told Coyote, "Move over a little." Coyote went over to the door again and sat down. This young man was sent after water and he spilt some water on Coyote intentionally because he envied Coyote's clothes. The son-in-law put food around and he came up to Coyote to give him some, but just as Coyote was reaching over to get it, he said to him, "Not you!" So Coyote got nothing to eat. After they had eaten, they smoked. When they had all smoked, Coyote wanted very much to have the pipe, but the son-in-law finished the pipe and hung it up high. Then Coyote got an idea. He thought, "I'll steal my son-in-law's pipe." He kept watching and when they fell asleep, he took the pipe, slipped out, and ran away. He ran until morning.

He saw the same house and thought, "There is Caucinsen. Oh, I might wake him up, but when he is awake, he'll be glad to get this pipe." Then he leaned his head against the door-poles and fell asleep. He woke up and saw someone going hunting and thought, "I was absent and Caucinsen has gotten a family." Just as he woke up, a man was walking by and he said, "You have a fine pipe in your mouth, Coyote." Then Coyote recognized the place he was in last night and knew that he was leaning against the house where he had stolen the pipe. He went in again and they sat. He said to his son-in-law, "I was afraid for your pipe, so I took it and stayed outdoors, so that no one in your family would steal it." He thought, "When the night comes, I'll run away in the other direction.

In the night when they fell asleep, Coyote took the pipe and ran away. He ran and got tired. He stopped, panting, and at his side someone was panting in the same way! They went down to a big lake. When they arrived at the shore, the son-in-law said to Coyote, "I'll be out in the water," but Coyote didn't hear him. Coyote threw the pipe out and it turned into an island. It is today an island still. Coyote said to his son-in-law, "If you are clever, this very island shall be your country, but if not, then this shore of the lake shall be your country." However, Coyote's son-in-law turned into a loon. Coyote took him and set him down on the water and said to him, "This water shall be your country." He said, "Well, dive!" The son-in-law dived and came out of the water again with a fish in his mouth. Coyote said to him, "Well, eat the fish!" The son-in-law swallowed it whole. Coyote asked him, "Was it good food?" and the son-in-law answered, "Yes, it was good food." Coyote said to him, "This shall be your food." Then they parted. That's the end.

Coyote and the Race

There lived a coyote. He had four children. The name of the youngest was Caucinsen, He-Washes-His-Ankle. The name of the next one was Pacelqeusen, He-Unjoints-At-His-Knee. The name of the next one was Kelttatalq, and the name of the eldest one was Miyaltko. The spring came and the children went out to get a vision. They went to the mountains and separated. They walked and they walked and the fall came. They had earlier fixed a date and a place where they should meet and exactly on that day, they met again. They went home and went in. Their father sat at home, so they sat down again. Coyote was very glad to see them again. They stayed home until the spring came, and then they disbanded again. The eldest brother said, "Here is the place where we will meet again." So they walked until the fall came and then they met again just where they had planned to meet. Then they walked home again. Their father sat there. He was very happy to see them. Then they stayed at home until spring came then they got ready.

Coyote had become lazy. He thought, "I'll go with them." As soon as they went out, Coyote ran out. He could not see anyone. He ran around in vain and when he got tired he went back into the house. He sat down again and he stayed home. When the fall arrived, they came back to him. He was glad to see his sons again. When the winter came, he made some sticks of wood for himself. Then he said to his sons, "One day you shall say to me, 'Let us go and see some people and gamble.'" He brought in his sticks. His sons did not pay any attention to him. Coyote turned around to his pillow and took out a wrapped bundle and unwrapped it. He took out a coyote-skin and put it on his head like a hat. He took out another coyote-skin and put it on. He took out one more coyote-skin and tied it around his waist. He took out one more coyote-skin and put it on too. He was watching his sons. They said, "What is our father going to do?" He took what he had made and took his sticks and put them down. All the while he watched his sons. Then Coyote sat down, took his sticks and struck with them and sang, "Poopoopoopoopoo." He got enough power and quit. He put them aside and saved them for another time.

Four years passed. The spring came and his sons said to him, "Get ready, Coyote, now we are going to see some people and gamble." Coyote was very happy. When he had got ready, they walked away. They walked and the evening came. They camped until the morning came and then they walked again. They went until noon, when they stopped, saying, "Let us stop here, our father is already getting thirsty. We'll get some water to drink."

Coyote was told, "Fill your pipe." He lit it and the eldest son ran back to their house. He was going after water. Just as Coyote had finished the pipe, the son came back. Coyote drank his fill and said, "Let us walk away from here." They walked and the evening came. They camped and the next morning walked farther on until noon. Then they said, "Now we'll stop. Our father has become thirsty. We'll get some water to drink." They said to him, "Fill your pipe." He filled it, lit it and the younger son left. Before Coyote had finished his pipe, the younger son came back. Coyote said, "He is very fast." Coyote drank his fill and said, "Now let us go from here." They walked and the evening came. Then the next morning they walked until noon. They said, "Our father has become thirsty so we'll get some water to drink." Coyote said, "Yes, there is a river nearby." They said to him, "Fill your pipe, Coyote." Coyote lit his pipe and Caucinsen ran away. Coyote had just enough time for a few puffs on his pipe when the son came back. He was the fastest one. Coyote drank his fill and they walked from there until evening came.

The next morning they said to Coyote, "This morning we'll arrive at a gambling place. When we arrive, don't behave like a fool." They said, "When we come in sight, they will say, 'Good, good, people are coming to gamble.' " Coyote and his sons were already in the race. Then they said to him, "You'll see one man run out, then another one, and that's the one who is going to run against us. When we are going to race, we'll take off our clothes and you gather our clothes."

Coyote took the clothes, walked down and sat down. He was told, "Do your best and smoke." Then Coyote took off his blanket, took all his tobacco, and scattered it over the blanket. Then he took the tobacco and filled his pipe. Then he smoked. They made a fire nearby and told him, "Don't quit smoking." People crowded around Coyote. As soon as he had finished the pipe, he filled it again. He just sat and smoked. He was told, "Do your best and smoke, Coyote. Your opponent is already half-way, and Caucinsen has not yet reached half-way. Do your best and smoke." He was told, "I'll be watching your race again." After a short while, he was poked and told, "Smoke, Coyote. Your opponent has just turned the corner and your Caucinsen is only half-way. Smoke, I'll go look at your racer." He went away in his turn. Coyote filled his pipe again and smoked again. The man came back and said, "Smoke! Caucinsen is already catching up. I'll go back and look at your racer." A short while later he came back and said, "Smoke, Coyote! Your Caucinsen is now very close to the other one. I'll go back and watch your racer." A short while later he came back again and said, "Smoke! I'll go back and watch your racer." He came back after awhile and said, "Smoke! Your racer has now caught up with his opponent." Just then he fell there — Coyote had won.

Caucinsen lay there panting, he was exhausted. Then the two racers went in again, but Caucinsen rested. Caucinsen said to Coyote, "Hurry now and take what you have won." "Go out," said Coyote. Then they all went out. "Come here, line up here," said Coyote. They lined up and Coyote sat. He said, "Bow your head to me." When they had bowed their heads to him, he said, "Sit down." They sat down. The chief was there with a big shock of hair on his forehead. Coyote said to them, "I'll talk to you." Then he said to the chief, "Now you shall stop killing people. Look, when people come here and race and lose, you kill them. If you don't listen, wherever I may be I'll come here immediately if you do this again and I will kill you. Now you have heard me, you are the chief."

When he had sharpened his knife, Coyote took the chief and cut off the chief's shock of hair. When he had cut it off, he said,

"Go, go in again." As soon as they had gone in again, Coyote said again, "Go out." Then they went out again. "Now, I'll go away," said Coyote. "I have already told you that if I hear that you kill them again, then wherever I may be I'll come back here and kill you." Coyote went up to the chief and asked him, "Did you hear me?" The chief said to Coyote, "Yes, I heard you." Then Coyote went back home. That's the end.

Coyote and His Teeth

Coyote took the road and was walking along. He saw a white, nice-looking house and he thought, "I'll go there." He went in. In the rear of the house he saw a ball of fat just lying there. As soon as he saw it, he wanted some so he walked toward it thinking, "I'll tell them some lies." He said to the people in the house, "We are four brothers." He thought, "If I bite four times, that'll be just enough." He bit a big piece, then he went out. He walked along, chewing and swallowing, and then turned around.

Coyote walked back on the road and went into the house again. The people said to him, "Hello," and told him to take one bite. Coyote said, "Hello. Perhaps my older brother has been in here?" They told him, "He has already been in here. You are not far behind." Then Coyote said, "We are hard up for food and are starving. My brothers will probably come here on the road. We have left each other." Coyote bit a big piece and then went out. First he turned onto the road again where he had been walking before. Then he took the road to the house again. They said, "Hello." He went in and they told him to take one bite. He asked, "Perhaps my older brothers have come in here?" They said to him, "Not very long ago they passed by here." He went and took a still bigger bite and then said, "Perhaps my younger brother will come in here and he'll be half dead from hunger." Then Coyote went out. He thought, "Now it'll be just enough when I take one more bite." Coyote walked on the road again.

The Meadowlark told the people in the house, "He is just one coyote and he is now going to eat up all your food." Coyote came back in, but the grease-ball had turned into stone. The people said, "Hello," and told him to take one bite. Coyote said, "Perhaps my older brothers have been here? They have left me." They told him, "They passed by here. You are not too far behind." Coyote thought his bite should be big this time. He bit, and crack! "Oh, I have done something wrong." He knew at once that all his teeth were gone. Coyote went out and he spat them out in his hand. They were all broken. He missed his teeth badly.

Coyote walked until he saw a house. He went in and sat down. The woman who was there was alone in the house. She made some food for him and put it down before him. He said to himself, "Oh, I wish I had my teeth to eat with." He cut some meat and put it in his mouth. It hurt very badly. He cut two pieces, but it hurt too much and he put it down again. She said to him, "Now say something." But he answered, "Hmmmm, I am not saying anything."

When evening came, someone knocked twice, opened the door in the rear, and came in. A man came in and brought two mountain sheep. The man said, "Oh, there sits my brother-in-law. Move over a bit, that is my place." There was another place to sit on the ground and Coyote sat down again. The door in the rear was opened again, and another man came in and threw down two mountain sheep. He said, "Oh, my brother-in-law sits there. Move over a bit, that is my place." There was still another place to sit and Coyote sat down.

The door opened again and another man came in carrying two mountain sheep. "Oh," the man said, "my brother-in-law sits there. Well, move over a bit, that is my place." Coyote dragged himself over to another place on the ground. He had already come close to the woman. The door opened, and a fourth man came in and threw down two mountain sheep. "Oh, there sits little Coyote." His older brothers said to him, "Be careful with what you say." The younger brother said to them, "It is my place he is sitting on. He is filling it with hair for me." His fellow-brothers said to him, "Stop bothering our brother-in-law with your talk." The youngest Coyote said, "Well, move

57

over there." Coyote sat down beside the woman and so got a wife.

Then they said to him, "Now tell us something." As Coyote was bashful because he had no teeth, he talked without opening his mouth. He said, "I don't like to talk." When they had cooked some food and given him some, he ate a little and quit. They said to him, "Now you must eat." But he answered, "No, it is my habit to eat little." They did not know what to think of him.

The next morning they went away one after another, but Coyote slept until daylight. As his wife watched him, he opened his mouth. "Oh, oh, but he has no teeth," she thought. Coyote's wife got up, and pulled some of the mountain-sheep's teeth. The woman took the mountain-sheep's teeth and put them all in Coyote's mouth, and so he had all his teeth again. Coyote was still asleep. She cooked some meat and then told Coyote to wake up. He got up and when he was awake, his food was put before him. Coyote said, "Oh, I wish I had my teeth." Then he took the knife and cut some meat. He put it in his mouth and chewed and chewed. "Oh," he thought, "it looks as if I have got my teeth back." He said to her, "I'll go out for a moment." He went out and touched them carefully. "Oh, I have my teeth again." Coyote went in again, sat down and ate. He ate very much. He had not eaten so much for a long time. The brothers came back and Coyote said, "Hahahaha." When she made some food he ate a great amount.

The next morning Coyote said, "I'll go hunting with you." They said, "No, we go across the lake and hunt." They said, "You'll come with us tomorrow." As soon as they had gone away, Coyote's wife tanned a skin. At dawn when she had finished it, they said to him, "Now, come with us, Coyote." As the morning came, they walked and walked and went down to a big lake. Coyote said, "Where is a boat for us?" They said to him, "No, we will fly."

When Coyote had left his wife had given him the skin she had tanned. When they came down to the water and he had asked them for a boat, they told him, "We'll fly." They said, "Well, put the skin down on the ground." They said to him, "You lie down on it there." Coyote was lifted up on it, and the others flew beside him. They flew, and just as they were over the middle of the lake, Coyote's travelling companions shouted, "Now he knows us! Drop him!" Coyote was happy, so happy that he shouted, "Woowoowoowoo!" The brothers said among themselves, "Oh, now he knows us," but they said to Coyote, "Shut up! We might drown." As a matter of fact, they dropped down toward the water, and they told Coyote not to yell. Coyote stopped shouting and they went up again. Finally, they hit the ground and began to walk.

They said to him, "You shall sit down here first. Don't shoot the small game." Then Coyote sat down and watched for the game. They had said, "Don't kill the small game." Then he felt something running all over him, so he took it, pinched it and threw it aside. A short while later, he took another one and threw it aside. They they came back to him and said, "Oh, but we told you awhile ago not to kill the small ones." He looked at them standing behind him watching. Then he turned around and saw many small ones. He told them, "Well, that is because I think they are very nice. It's because where I come from, they kill all kinds of game, and I kill the small ones because they're going to use their shirts and because there are so many of them." One of the brothers was told, "Go and bring him something he can kill." The brother went away and after awhile he put two mountain-sheep down before him. Coyote got two mountain-sheep. Then they all crossed the lake again and came back to their home.

The next morning Coyote's wife said to him, "You shall not go with them. In just four days you may go with them, Coyote. When you know them well, then you'll fly with them." He stayed home one day and the next morning said, "I'll go with them," and although his wife told him not to go he said, "I'll go with them now." Then she gave him the mountain-sheep skin and said, "Go with them." Then they walked a long time and went down to the lake.

The brothers asked Coyote, "Where is the thing you have brought with you?" He took it out from under his arm and spread it on the ground. Coyote lay down on it. Then they all flew, and just as they were over the middle of the lake, Coyote shouted, "Uuuu." "Oh, drop him!" said one of them, "drop him, he knows us already." They dropped him. Coyote made somersault after somersault in the air and fell down into the water. His tail was sticking out of the water. The oldest brother turned around and grabbed Coyote's tail and flew up. It came off. But there was still a little tail-stump left, so he came back and grabbed that too and it came off. When the stump came off, he said to his brothers, "Let us run away." They went ashore.

In the house where Coyote lived, his arrow broke and fell down. The woman thought, "Now they have killed my husband." She got ready. She took out all her veins and tied them up in her hat saying, "Now you are through, my brothers." They ran. One of them said, "Now she is on her way here." They fled. The oldest of them said, "I'll stop here." He took a place under a tree. After a short while, he saw her coming. She said to her oldest brother, "You have to die. You harmed me through my husband." Then she shot him, went up to him and broke his neck. Then she walked on from there.

She pursued the rest of them in order to kill them. They ran on until another one got tired and said to his brothers, "Now, I'll stay here. Our older brother has already been killed. When you get tired, don't leave one another, but stand together in one place." Then the younger brothers walked away. From his place, the older brother saw their sister coming toward him. She said to him, "Why does he stand? You harmed me through my husband." Then she shot him, went up to him and broke his neck.

The two who were left went far off where they were told by the Meadowlark, "It is quite useless for you to shoot at her body. She'll get close up to you and throw off her hat. When she comes close to you, and when she throws off her hat, it's her hat you shoot at." Then they saw her coming and she said to them, "You have to die, why do you stand?" When she approached them and when she threw off her hat, they fell upon it and shot at her hat. She said, "Don't shoot at it and you shall live." They pierced the hat with arrows and she died.

60

Coeur d'Alene Myths

Chief Child of the Root
Origin of Indian Tribes
Coyote Overpowers Sun
Coyote Loses His Eyes
Story of Lynx
Dog Husband
Catbird
Skunk and Fisher
Thunder

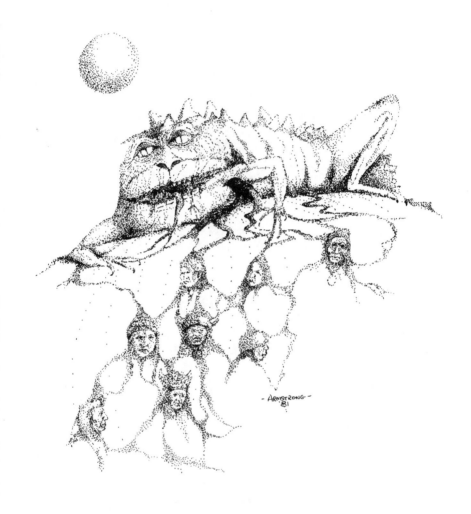

Chief Child of the Root

An old woman lived with her daughter who had a baby boy. Every day the daughter went out to gather the roots of plants and every day she came back with a great many of the roots. She baked them and the family ate them and the boy grew. The mother always went out alone to gather roots, leaving the boy with his grandmother. One day when he was quite large he asked, "Where is my father?" His grandmother said, "You are pitiable, you have no father." "Why have I no father?" he asked. "He has been dead a long time." The boy asked, "What was his name?" "He had none," answered the grandmother. Then the boy took a stick and threatened, "If you don't tell me who my father was I will kill you." "You are a Child of the Root," confessed the grandmother.

The boy was sad, so lay down and covered himself with his blanket. All day he lay like that. In the evening when his mother came back and saw him lying as he was she thought, "I

The boy was sad, so lay down and covered himself with his blanket. All day he lay like that. In the evening when his mother came back and saw him lying as he was she thought, "I suppose his grandmother has been telling him tales." She said nothing but made signs that she was going to club her mother. After she had cooked the roots for his grandmother, she said, "Come, we are going to eat!" The boy paid no attention. She and her mother ate but the boy would not join them. The next day the same thing happened, he refused to eat. The mother went out to gather more roots. After she was gone the boy got up and said to his grandmother, "I am leaving you for good."

He went out to the edge of the water and sat down. He sang, "Ahoiye xiya, Chief Child of the Root, xeya, xeya." He washed his face, his head, and his entire body. He reached into the water and took out the throat of a monster fish. He made a canoe of it, got into it and rowed away singing his song. He heard someone who said, "Chief Child of the Root, give me a ride. We'll see the whole world even to where the river enters the sea." "All right, I'll give you a ride," he said.

However, when the passenger, who was Pestle Boy, got into the boat, he began to jump up and down. "You might break my canoe," the Chief said. "Here, I'll fix a paddle for you to sit on." He fixed it but Pestle Boy continued to jump up and down until Child of the Root dumped him into the water. "You will no longer eat people. They will use you for a pestle," he decreed.

The Chief went on singing. Suddenly he saw a tree burning. Someone fell off it into the fire. He thought, "That person will die." He hurried ashore and looked and found Foolhen feeling her eyebrows which were all red and blistered from the fire. Chief Child of the Root said to her, "What's the matter?" "Well, Chief, I was gathering black moss." Chief Child said, "Don't do that any more, you might die. If you get hungry for it again, fly up to a tree and eat it raw right off the tree. Eat it all up, as much as you want. Don't have a house anymore and don't try to cook it!" "Thank you, Chief," she said. Before this she had gathered the moss and put it under her wing. Then she set the tree afire and cooked the moss by falling into the fire herself.

He went off again. Suddenly a rabbit jumped into the water. Chief Child of the Root clubbed it, put it into his canoe, and went on. Then he heard the sound of tramping and saw Fisher who said, "Chief Child of the Root, give me my game." Chief Child replied, "No, I didn't see it!" Fisher jumped into the water. "If you don't show me where it is I'll slap you with my tail." Chief Child of the Root said, "Go ahead, slap me with your tail!" Fisher jumped about in the water and swam until he got close to the Chief. Then he turned around and slapped the water with his tail. He got the Chief all wet. Then the Chief hit him and he died. He put Fisher into the canoe with the rabbit and paddled on.

The Chief came to a place where there were many children and went ashore. When the children saw him they ran into the house. Their mother asked, "What is the matter?" but they did not answer. Chief Child of the Root came in. The mother looked at him and said, "Chief, you honor our humble home." He sat down. "We are pitiable," she said, "we have nothing to offer you to eat." No, I am not hungry," he said. Soon she told the children to look for their father. They looked for him but soon came back and reported, "Our father is gone." The mother said, "I guess he is hunting, he'll be back. Maybe he has killed something, then we can eat."

The Chief looked around and saw a lot of rabbit skins. He thought, "They must like rabbits." He told the children to get the one from his canoe. They went to the canoe and saw their father lying dead in it. They cried, "It's our father lying dead there in the canoe!" The mother said, "I suppose he was doing something foolish again." When the Chief found he had killed their father, he said, "Go get him and he will come back to life again." The children brought him up and laid him down. The Chief stepped over him. Fisher got up and said, "Oh Chief, you find us humble." These were the first words he uttered.

The Chief went on. He saw a house with smoke coming out. He thought, "That's where I'll eat." He went ashore. There was a good fire burning in the house but the people seemed to be gone. He saw little owls hanging all over the walls. In the middle was a large one, nicely beaded. He went over and took it down. As he was going out with it all the owls cried out, "He is taking our chief," and came down from the wall and pierced him all over his body. "Don't do that! I guess it must be your chief I took." He hung up the ornamented owl and went out, then he set the house afire. As he went off he heard the owls crying, "Yar, yar, yar!" He said, "Don't be man-eaters anymore. You'll be used for making moccasins."

Chief Child went on. Farther on he saw something which looked like a house and went in. No one was at home but there was a fire. He saw combs hanging all over the walls. A large one decorated with beads was in the center. He thought, "I'll comb myself with that nice one." As he went out with it the others cried out, "Our chief is being taken away," and they all came at him and combed him. "Oh! It's your chief? I'll hang him back again." Chief Child hung it on the wall, went out and set fire to the house. As he went on he heard the combs shrieking. "Don't be man-eaters," he shouted. "You'll be used to comb hair."

He went on and saw another house. Inside there was a fire and many bladders were hung on the walls. In the middle of one wall was a fine large one. "I'll take that for my own use." He thought, "I'll keep my kinnikinnick in it or I can use it for my powder." He took it, but just as he went on he heard crying. "He took our chief!" He felt them all bumping him and some blowing him in the face. "Stop that! If it's your chief, I'll put him back," and he hung it up again. Then he went out, struck a light and burned the house. He heard the bursting of many tight skins as he went on. "No more will you be man-eaters. Hereafter you'll be used for storing tobacco."

At another house the walls were hung with lassos with a large fine one in the center. Chief Child had no more than taken it down when all the rest cried out, "It's our chief!" They came down and lassoed him and so he put it back. He destroyed the house with fire saying, "No more will you be man-eaters. You'll have to make your living. When people want food they will use you to trap their game."

The Chief went on and saw Kingfisher sitting on a tree. As he was looking Kingfisher dived. Soon he came up holding his hair in front with both hands. He ran into his house and soon came back with a bucket. He filled it, ran and built a fire. Chief Child of the Root thought, "I had better look into this."

The Chief crept and looked in. He saw Kingfisher holding his hair and washing it in the bucket. He was wiping his hands on his hair because the fish smell was all that there was left of his catch and he was making soup of it. The Chief went back to his boat and returned as if he had seen nothing. "You honor a humble home, Chief, but I am very poor," Kingfisher said when he saw the Chief. The bucket was boiling with the water Kingfisher had washed from his hair. "I am poor, I have no other food. If I had something to eat you could eat with me." Chief Child of the Root said, "I am not hungry." The kettle boiled and got white on top. Kingfisher set it down and said, "Stay and have a drink of soup." The Chief took a cupful and drank. He had never tasted such good soup. He drank it all. "You should have had something to eat," said Kingfisher. "I guess you saw me when I dived for a fish. I got hold of him but he slipped away because my nails are too short. Why is it they are so close to the flesh?"

The Chief took Kingfisher's hands, put something like a

cat's claw on them and they became long. "You can do anything you want with them now." Then he opened the bird's mouth, took a knife and cut his bill in several places so it was like a file. Then he said, "Go try it. Get a fish."

Kingfisher went out to his tree and sat until he saw a fish. Then he dived. He got his fish, bit it and held it fast. He took it back to the house. "Thank you, Chief," he said. He got a bucketful of water and cooked the fish. He was very grateful. Then the Chief said, "Now I must go." "No, stay and eat," said Kingfisher. "I drank some soup," the Chief replied. "You eat what you have, eat it all. Then fly, don't live in a house. Go sit on a willow and watch the water. Don't take the big fish or the small ones, but the ones that are just big enough for a meal. Don't cook your food but eat it raw." "Thank you, Chief, thank you," said Kingfisher.

Then Chief went on. He saw a fishhawk jump into the water and come up with clasped hands. This person also ran into the house, brought out a bucket, filled it and went in to make a fire. The Chief watched and saw him wringing the ends of his fingers in the pail. He withdrew and came up openly to Fishawk's house.

"Oh, Chief, you find me humble. I am poor," Fishhawk said. When the kettle boiled Fishhawk game the Chief some soup. It was very good. Then he said, "If it weren't for my fingernails I would have plenty to eat. I guess you saw how I tried to catch a fish." Chief Child of the Root said, "Let me see your hand." The Chief treated the nails as he had Kingfisher's and they became long. Fishhawk tried them and came gleefully back with many fish. "Thank you, Chief. Stay and eat with me," he invited. "No, I have eaten. You eat it by yourself. Then fly. Don't have a house and don't cook, eat your food raw. Take only one fish and eat it all." Thank you, Chief."

The Chief paddled on to where the brook ran into a river. There stood a man aiming a spear. He saw that one of the man's legs was extremely thin and wondered why it was. He thought, "I ought to see it right." He jumped out of his canoe, turned himself into a salmon, and swam up to Splinter Leg. Splinter Leg speared him, but Chief Child ran off so the spearhead broke the line. Splinter Leg cried, "Oh! It hurts after all my suffering."

The Chief got into his canoe and speared a salmon with the same spearhead. Then he went back, but Splinter Leg was gone. The Chief went to his house, peeped in, and saw Splinter Leg cutting another spearhead out of his own legbone and crying. The Chief drew back, then walked in. Splinter Leg covered his leg with his blanket and said. "Weak, poor, and pitiful you find me, Chief. I have nothing to eat." "I am not hungry," said the Chief. "I would have something for you to eat because just as you came in sight I speared a salmon, but my line broke and carried off my spearhead."

"I saw a fine big salmon lying in the water with a spearhead in it," said the Chief. "That must have been yours. Go get it from my canoe." As Splinter Leg got up he quickly drew his blanket around his leg. He brought the salmon back, cooked it, and served it. They ate. The Chief kept watching his leg, but Splinger Leg took care not to expose it.

After they ate, the Chief proposed a hoop and stick game, but Splinter Leg refused, saying he did not know how to play. "All right," the Chief said. Then Splinter Leg suddenly changed his mind. "Oh, well, let's play. What will we bet?" "Your blanket," the Chief replied. The Chief won. Then Splinter Leg bet his shirt and lost again.

The Chief could see that he did not want to give up the blanket. "Come now, give me your blanket." When Splinter Leg did not give the Chief the blanket immediately, the Chief hit him with a stick and broke his leg. Then he took the blanket off Splinter Leg's leg. "You have made me more pitiable," Splinter Leg said as the Chief looked at his leg. "Why did you cut bone from your leg?" the Chief asked. "Because I needed a spearhead carved of bone," Splinter Leg replied. Then he began to cry, "Now you've made me much worse." "I only did it because I mean to fix it," the Chief replied.

The Chief saw that while the one leg was as thin as could be, the other was normal. He rubbed the thin leg and smoothed it and it became as good as new. Then he took the blanket and handed it to its owner. "Here is your blanket." "Go ahead, take it," said Splinter Leg as he took off his shirt. "No, you keep them," the Chief said. "Thank you, thank you," Splinter Leg said. The Chief went out and came back with something in his hand. It was an elk antler. "After this make your spearhead of this. Don't cut yourself for it." "Thank you, thank you," repeated Splinter Leg.

Again the Chief Child paddled away. After going a long way he saw many people. They saw him too. "He is coming, Chief Child of the Root," they cried. Two of them came to meet the Chief and carried him in by the arms. The chief of the people said, "I have two daughters, they are yours."

It was so crowded that Toad was pushed way back and could see nothing. This always happened to Toad because she was so ugly. "I must see him too," said Toad stretching as high as she could. "What's the use of your seeing him, an ugly thing like you?" the people around her said. "It's true, I suppose," agreed Toad ruefully.

Toad then went out for water. She sprinkled water from the sky. She went into her house and sat down patiently waiting. It rained, then it poured. Everybody went home. It was so wet in the houses no one could lie down. Chief Child of the Root tipped his canoe over to lie under it, but soon it was wet there too. He got up and saw a light far off. He went in the direction of the light, which was in Toad's house. She had a nice fire and everything was dry and comfortable.

"You are dry, my grandmother. Why are you not wet?" Toad laughed, "Now I can see you close-up even if I am ugly." The Chief Child said, "You are dry, my grandmother." "I'm not your mother's mother." "What are you then, my father's mother?" "No." "Are you my younger sister?" "No." "Are you my daughter?" "No." Chief Child got up. He looked back as he was going out and asked one parting question, "Are you my wife? What are you to me?"

Toad jumped up and landed above the Chief's nose right between his eyes. He tried to pull her off but the skin stretched. He said to the people, "Come get this toad off me." They came to help him. They tried to cut off the toad with a knife, but to no avail.

Coyote cried, "All right, let's talk this over." They came together for a council. Coyote addressed the meeting first. "We ought to have a sun. At night we ought to have a moon. I'll be the moon myself." Robin said, "I'll be the sun." At night

69

whenever anyone did anything Coyote announced the act to all the people. In the daytime the sun came up. It was so hot the people did nothing but swim. They decided that Coyote was utterly no good because he spied on everything everyone did. They pulled Coyote down and threw him away. Robin was too hot so she suffered the same fate. Then said the Chief Child of the Root, "I will be the moon. I'll go far off so you can't see the Toad on my face very well." Helldiver's child who has only one eye said, "I'll be a good sun for you because I can't see very well. I will not be too light or hot." "All right," said the Chief Child.

Now you know about the Chief Child of the Root.

Origin of Indian Tribes
(From Parts of Monster)

Rabbit had a house near Grizzly Bear's. Grizzly was always starving and Rabbit always had to feed him. Besides eating everything he wished, Grizzly always wanted to take some food along home with him. Then he became so greedy that he thought he would kill Rabbit and get all the food. "Let's play," he proposed. Rabbit said, "We are no children to be playing." "Oh, come on, let's play. Let's go swimming."

When they were in the water Grizzly said, "Let's splash. Let me be first." He took water and threw it at Rabbit, then laughed. Rabbit took a big spoon made of elk antler. While Grizzly was laughing he filled it with water and threw it down Grizzly's throat. Grizzly almost choked, but Rabbit ran away into his house before Grizzly recovered. He threw Grizzly's food out at him and saw him eat it greedily. Then Grizzly laughed again, "We are only playing," but to himself he said, "I'm going to shoot him in the eye."

Rabbit took a bladder, blew it up and put it in his eye. Grizzly shot at him and the bladder burst. Grizzly laughed, "My, isn't that fun!" Then came Rabbit's turn. He shot and put out Grizzly's eye. Grizzly growled in fury and pain, but Rabbit ran home. Then Rabbit ran into the timber and soon came to the house where a wicked old woman lived with her daughter and son-in-law. The husband of the girl was gone, so Rabbit killed the girl. He took a knife and began to skin her. As he did so he asked the old woman, "Are my ears getting longer?" "Yes," she said. Then as he cut the daughter down the back he asked, "Is my fat showing?" "Yes," the old woman was compelled to answer.

The girl had an understanding with her husband when they first got married. She had told him, "If one of your arrows breaks when you are hunting then you will know I am dead." He had told her, "If ever your digging stick breaks when you are digging camas you will know I am dead."

Now when the husband was out hunting he was warned of his wife's disaster by the breaking of his arrow. He hurried home. "Mother-in-law, what does this mean?" he asked. "Rabbit came in, killed our daughter, cut her open and went away again."

Rabbit had escaped into the timber but the man went after him. Rabbit made all kinds of tracks in the timber so the man could not track him easily, but nevertheless he followed. Then Rabbit put cooked camas down at intervals. This was so the man would be delayed by picking it up to eat. Finally Rabbit came to the open prairie. Just as he got a good start forward, he ran into Coyote. Rabbit said, "You shouldn't delay me this way, a monster is chasing me."

Coyote took up some jointgrass, pulled the joints apart and hid Rabbit in it. Rabbit was shaking with fear, so Coyote blew the jointgrass so it looked as if it was shaking in the wind. Then he consulted his powers. The first one said, "The monster who is after you has a dog, the Grizzly Bear, so I'll be your dog and my name will be the same. I'll be very small." The second power said, "I'll be a knife at the back of your dog's head." The third said, "I'll give you the power to gobble everything up."

Then they saw the monster coming with his dog. "Did you see what I am chasing?" he asked roughly. Coyote asked, "What are you chasing?" "A rabbit," replied the monster. "I didn't see him," Coyote said. The monster said, "Maybe he passed before I came." The monster's dog began to growl. "Be quiet, Grizzly!" said Coyote to his own dog. "Why, we call our pets by the same name!" said the monster.

Coyote answered, "Aha! My father and his father, then his father and his father had the same name for their dogs." Then the monster became angry and walked toward Coyote's pet. He said, "Make your dog stop growling or we might kill you." Coyote said, "You stop yours." "You better listen to me, he will kill you," the monster warned. Coyote laughed, "We might kill you." "Oh, no," said the monster. Then Coyote proposed, "Let's let our dogs fight."

So they turned the dogs loose and they fought: Coyote's dog was bitten and stepped on, but Coyote just laughed. He called, "What is the matter with you, Grizzly? Why don't you put your head under him?" and he laughed again. Again he egged him on. The Coyote's dog crawled under Grizzly dog and ripped his stomach open with the knife behind his head. The Grizzly dog fell dead.

The monster mourned for his dog, but Coyote said, "It's too bad. I told you to call off your dog when they started to fight. I saw they were mad." The monster retorted, "Shut up! I'll gobble you up! Coyote answered, "Do you mean that you will gobble *me* up? I'll gobble *you* up. Let's see if we can gobble up that tree. You try first."

The monster tried, but left about three feet of the stump standing. Coyote laughed, "I thought you were smart. Now look at me!" He gobbled and when he was through not a splinter of the tree was left. "Now look," said Coyote. "That is the way real gobblers gobble. Let's go and gobble that cliff. You go first." The monster gobbled at it but when he had done his best some rocks were left. Coyote laughed. He gobbled and not a pebble was left. "You are not like me," he bragged, "I am the smart one!" "I might gobble you up," said the monster. "All right," said Coyote, try it!"

Before Coyote could look he found himself inside the monster's stomach. There were lots of people there playing games. Some were playing the stickgame, others cards, still others were dancing a war dance. Coyote said to them, "What's the matter with you all? You are pitiful. Don't you know you are in the belly of a monster? I am going out of here. Get yourselves ready. Soon I'll be back, then I'll fix it so you can come out."

He tickled the monster's heart until he was spat out and landed far away. Coyote picked up a stick to make a hoop and continued making hoops as he talked to the monster. "Your insides show you are a good gambler. You are a card player." Coyote had made a hoop the size of the monster's mouth and was now fashioning two smaller ones the size of his nostrils. "You are a good war dancer."

The monster answered, "I vomited you up because you are no good. I eat only good things." Coyote said, "You only think so. You eat mice. I am the one who eats really good things." The monster said, "Just a minute ago I got through eating two nice, neat, good-looking people." Coyote said, "I was the one who ate those two." "If that's true vomit them out," the monster replied angrily. "Come," said Coyote, "sit down there and close your eyes. I'll close mine and we will see what we can vomit. You do it first!"

The monster vomited two people and Coyote four mice. Coyote threw the mice in front of the monster and put the people on his side. Then he said, "Let's open our eyes." Coyote laughed, "Those nice-looking ones are the ones I ate." The monster could not believe his eyes. "They are the ones I ate. I never did eat mice." "Look where they are," said Coyote. "They're on your side." "I'll gobble you up!" shouted the monster. "You're a mouse-eater!" replied Coyote. Coyote had the hoops in his hand and held them flat. "All right, go on, gobble me up," teased Coyote.

Again in a twinkling he was in the monster's stomach. "Hello!" he said to the people. "Wait till I run out, then you can get out too." He ripped open the stomach and it was light again. The people ran out while Coyote cut off the monster's heart. Then he set the large hoop so it would hold the mouth open and the smaller ones in the nostrils. Everyone came out. The monster died and Coyote ran off.

Coyote went back to the jointgrass where Rabbit was hiding and took him out. Rabbit was glad to be free. Then Coyote told Rabbit to cut the monster up. Rabbit cut him all up and Coyote took the pieces and threw them about. He threw a leg and said, "You will become the Blackfoot Indians, you will be tall." He threw a rib saying, "You will be the Nez Perce, you will have good heads." The paunch became the Gros Ventre, "You will have big bellies." Then he threw the heart. "You'll be the Coeur d'Alene, you'll be courageous." He threw all the pieces away. Then he wiped his hands on some grass and threw the grass away. "You will be the Spokane, you will be poor," he decreed.

That is the end of my road. Now you know how the Indian tribes came about.

Coyote Overpowers Sun

Coyote and Antelope lived together. Each had four children. The Coyote children had names, but the Antelope children had none. Every morning Coyote's children went into the sweathouse and Antelope's children went away. In four days they returned. Then Coyote's children went away and Antelope's children went into the sweathouse to sweat. They did that for a month and then they all went far away. They came to a place where there were many people. At night the oldest Coyote stopped nearest the people. Then the second, the third, and finally the youngest took up his place. Then the oldest Antelope took his place, and the others arranged themselves in order according to age.

Sun, who was chief of the people, had a valuable disk that the Antelopes wanted. It lay in the chief's house, so Coyote's oldest child went in and took it. When the people found it was gone they cried out and began to chase him. Just as they were about to kill him he rolled it to his next younger brother. In this way each Coyote got it and passed it to the next, although he was killed in doing so. The youngest Coyote passed it to the oldest Antelope. Each Anthelope passed it to his brother and they all escaped because they could outrun the Sun's people.

Coyote and Antelope had been listening for the return of their children. Now they heard the cry of mourning and heard the Antelope children announcing, "Oh, you have no children anymore, Coyote." Antelope asked, "They said 'Coyote?' "

"No," said Coyote, "they said 'Antelope.' " As they were arguing the same cry came again. Each insisted it was announcing the misfortune of the other.

Finally Antelope said, "My children are not lazy enough to be killed." Coyote retaliated, "Are they not my children who go to rocky places and eat nothing but rosehips for four days at a time?" Then Antelope put a stick in the fire and when it was well burned hit Coyote making marks around his eyes. Coyote burned a stick and just as Antelope ran out hit him with it at the root of his tail and one his legs.

Coyote left Antelope's house. He cried all the time. Then Antelope said to his children, "Whenever he stops crying give him the sun's disk. His children are the ones who really got it." Coyote kept on crying. He did not sleep for about four days. By that time his cry, "My children," had become very faint. Antelope said, "Go and see how Coyote is." Some went. They pulled aside the rush mat which served as a curtain and saw nothing, but the crying continued weakly. They looked around for Coyote and found that he had left long ago. He had left his spittle crying in the fire.

When the Antelope came looking for Coyote they saw him running with the precious disk. They followed him to the cliff over which Spokane Falls runs. When Coyote got there he said, "Four times I will pretend to throw it over the cliff. The fourth time I will really throw it into the river." Each time he raised it he sang, "The precious disk," but he did not let it go. After three times he said. "Only once more then I'll let you go. Then you'll stay for good."

Meanwhile, the Antelopes were coming nearer. Just as he let it go, one caught it exclaiming, "How can you ever pay for it?" Coyote answered, "What did you pay for it when you had this valuable thing?" The Antelope took it. Coyote kept on crying. He went home, but he did not eat or sleep. He just cried for some days. One day at sunset he stopped crying and said, "That's enough." Antelope said, "You smarty of a Coyote!" Then Coyote sang,

> "I ought not to be a woman.
> Why should I soil my eyes with crying.
> Go and sing, my aunties."

"Now I am going to avenge my children." Antelope said again, "That smarty of a Coyote!"

Coyote left. All night he serenaded his aunties, the little mice. Just about daylight he said to his aunties, "In just a month after I have gone you will think me dead." As he went out he said, "Good day, my aunties," and left. He walked and walked in broad daylight. He thought by walking east he would get to where the sun was. The sun saw him and said, "You sly one! You think you are going to take revenge and you walk in plain sight."

Each day this happened. One day Coyote saw two nicely smoothed little sticks in the road. He stepped on them and they broke. The sticks were really Meadowlark's legs. "You broke my legs and I was going to tell you a story." Coyote answered, "I have business to attend to now." Meadowlark said, "What do you have to worry so about?" "Oh, all right, tell me a story and I will fix your legs for you," said Coyote.

He put the bones in place and smoothed them. Then Meadowlark said, "Why do you go around in the daytime when the sun is out? He can see you walking around. Don't walk any more in the daytime, but only at night. At daylight lie down in a hole in the ground and sleep. About sunset get up and walk." Coyote said, "Thank you."

He rewarded Meadowlark by putting around her neck a black medal on a black string which had belonged to Bluebird. Now Coyote travelled only at night. At dawn he lay down until the sun was gone. The sun wondered, "I wonder where he is. Maybe he is lying down."

Then Coyote saw the spring where the sun paused to drink every day at noon. He consulted his own magic powers. "Tell me what to do right away." They said, "He never passes by that spring without stopping. Always at noon he stops to drink." Coyote went over to the spring. He saw two holes where the sun placed his knees as he bent to drink. His powers told him, "Opposite those holes dig two for yourself. At dinner time when he comes down he will stop there. He will descend but will not touch the ground. Don't attack him until he comes down." One power gave Coyote a small knife like a paring knife and the other gave him something to shoot with. The third power held him back when the sun pretended he was coming to earth.

The next day the sun rose. He said, "Coyote, whoever seeks revenge must lie down." Coyote said, "He saw me already, I may as well be walking." But his powers said, "No, he is only pretending. After a while he will come closer." Coyote saw something hanging down from the sun's head. His powers said, "That is his heart. That is what you must cut off."

Up again went the sun. "Let me get him," said Coyote. "No, he'll soon come very close," and his power held him back. Once more it came down. "I am going to shoot at him," Coyote said. "No, you would only shoot in vain. He would not die. You must cut off his bangs. Only then will he die."

The next time the sun touched the ground, looked around, and there was the water. He reached across the spring and supported himself, then drank. Coyote was lying there near the sun's heart. His power said, "Grab it!" Coyote pulled it and bit it. One power handed him the little knife and said, "Cut it!" He cut it and the sun fell down and died. It became dark. Then all the Indians said, "Now Coyote had murdered someone."

Coyote went off. He went very far and still he stumbled over sun. He felt around saying, "This is the one I killed." Every time he stepped he stumbled over the body because it was so dark. Again he asked his powers what to do. They said, "Put down that thing you are holding in your hand." He put it down and it became light again.

As for Coyote, he fell from the cliff and died. He got up after a while, but he fell again. He found he had broken his leg. He took a piece of willow, chewed it, and stuffed it into the hole in his bone. He ate off the end of the other piece of bone and stuffed chewed willow in that. Then he pressed the two ends together. Some children saw him do this. "Coyote is eating himself," they called. Coyote called back, "Come fix it for me! I broke my leg." Two of the children came. Coyote grabbed one of them and twisted his mouth. He did the same to the other. They could say nothing but, "Tsu, tsu, tsu." They had become crossbills.

Coyote went on and came on a man throwing up his eyes. He would run and say, "My eyes, come back again!" Then they would drop into his sockets again. Coyote said, "My gr-gr-gr-grandfather knew that trick, too. Do you think you are the only one who knows it?" Coyote took out his eyes and threw them up. "Come drop back, my eyes!" But the man ran and caught them and Coyote had no eyes.

Coyote went on. He heard someone say, "Coyote is going to fall off." Coyote was pretending he could see and would not look at the man. He thought, "Maybe he sees a deer." He asked, "Is it a deer you see?" The other said, "What, what? Where?" Coyote answered, "There, don't you see it?" Coyote took him by the head, "There it is. Come, I'll aim your eye. I'll point right at it."

He took hold of the man's head and aimed it, then pulled out his eyes and put them into his own sockets. He could see again. He threw the man over the cliff and he became Catbird. Coyote said, "Whenever anyone hears you that person will become lonesome."

Coyote Loses His Eyes

Coyote was going along and he came to a house where there were many pheasant children. It was dusty in there and the mouths of the children were dirty. Coyote asked, "What are you doing?" "We are baking berries." "Where are they?" "There in that sack." Coyote said, "Go, get me a sack. I am going to bake some."

They brought him a sack. He prepared the oven, put the berries in, covered them, and put a fire on top. "Eat so you grow fast," he told the children. He ate also and asked when he had finished, "Did you have enough?" "Yes." "Who is your father?" asked Coyote. "He-Spits-On-the-Head." "And your mother?" "She-Darts-Between-the-Legs." "Bring another sack," ordered Coyote. Then he killed the pheasant children and arranged them around the fire and went off. He sang, "They don't make their children mind."

The Pheasants were picking berries and heard him singing for about a mile. The man said, "I suppose he has done

78

something to our children. You stay here and I'll go see what is wrong." He flew home and found his children all dead. He went back and told his wife. "It's terrible about our children," she said. "Let's follow Coyote."

They flew after Coyote. "Pheasants' children don't mind," sang Coyote as he went along. The Pheasants took a road which ran right along the edge of a cliff and waited there for Coyote. He came along singing.

The man said, "I'll be the first, I'll fly at his face." When he was right over Coyote he swooped down and spat on him. As Coyote jumped the mother flew between his legs. Coyote was so frightened he fell over the cliff. The Pheasants went home. It was awful to see the children and the parents cried. They picked up the remains, washed them, and stepped over them. Then the children became alive.

Coyote looked and saw that if he had taken one more step he would have fallen over the cliff. He had eyes again but they were very small. As he went on, he saw a woman sitting in the trail. He said, "Move aside!" She paid no attention. He said, "I told you to move over. Are you dead?" She sat still, so he went near to her ear and shouted, but she did not answer. He went still closer and said, "Are you blind?"

Coyote was thirsty, so he went down to the spring and drank. He found some nettles and pulled some out. Then he went back and said, "If you don't move I'll touch you with these." When she didn't move, he touched her with them. "Don't! I'll move," she said. "Only don't touch me with them." Coyote began to sing, "If you don't move I am going to touch you with nettles." She said, "Stop it! I'll move. I'm going with you." "Why should you want to go with me? Why didn't you say so long ago?"

They went along together. One night they heard singing and Coyote said, "Let's go see what it is." The woman said, "No, we are going on." Coyote said, "Let's go just for a little while." She said, "No!" and went on without him. Coyote followed the sound to a big lodge and went in. People were dancing there so he danced, too. He saw hanging bladders full of fat and thought, "I will blow out the light. They used to dance in the dark."

Coyote blew out the light, found the bladder and jumped up at it. Instead of fat he found only rocks. He tried another bladder. It made a noise like a bag of rocks. "Light the light," he said. When it was lit again he saw there were no people. Instead, everywhere he moved there were rocks. They came closer and closer together. "Where are you, my partners?" he cried, but no one answered. He cried and cried but finally he could not even move his head because of the rocks.

In the morning he heard animals pecking. "Come over and help me out. Peck me out of here," said Coyote. Woodpecker pecked around his nose. "You are pitiful," he said. Coyote said, "Peck out my eyes so I can see people." "All right," Woodpecker answered, "I will get you out." He pecked all around Coyote's eye. At night he said, "It is dark now. I will leave you, but I will come back in the morning."

Woodpecker went home and tied up his head. "What's the matter?" asked his wife. "I bet you were pecking at that Coyote." "No, I was pecking at something to eat. All day I was busy at it and that is why my head aches," replied Woodpecker. The next day Woodpecker worked again. About noon he got to Coyote's eye. Then Coyote could see with one eye. "Now you are all right. You can see again. My head aches terribly, so I will leave you."

Coyote could see the sky. Soon he heard a noise and saw Buzzard flying above him. "My, you are ugly!" said Coyote. "I shouldn't be looking at you. You are black, your legs are rough, your eyes are white, your nose is long." Just as Coyote said "Ugly," Buzzard swooped down angrily and pecked out his eye. Coyote set up a howl. "I can't see any more." He took his head in his hands and moved the other eye to the hole, but Buzzard pecked it out too.

Then the woman, who was sitting where Coyote had left her, threw out her belt and caused the rocks to scatter. Then she led Coyote away. Soon she saw a deer and said, "There's a deer. I wish there were a man here to shoot it." Coyote said, "Am I not a man? Fix an arrow for me and aim it. You hold it still and tell me when it is ready, then I'll shoot."

She did as he directed and he killed the deer. Then he praised himself, "My, I am a pretty good shot! I killed that deer all right." The woman said, "You shot a tree." "Oh! I was just talking," replied Coyote. "Come, let's get the arrow." She took it out of the deer and put it away. Then she led Coyote around in a circle all day. Finally Coyote said, "Aren't we near the place where we can go through? It seems as if we were going the wrong way. I don't know why we're not there, we've already gone over many hills." Then the woman told him, "No, we've only gone over one that was hard to walk over."

She made a big fire. Then she said, "I am going to fix some medicine for your eyes." Coyote sat there patiently. She cut up the deer and broke the bone at the knee. "My, it sounds good!" thought Coyote. "She is breaking the deer's leg." "I just broke a stick," said the woman. "Oh, I was only wishing," answered Coyote. She began to roast the liver and Coyote exclaimed, "My, that sounds good!" "The wood is wet, that is the reason it makes that snapping noise," she said. "I was only saying that," Coyote said. She took some fat and tied it up and said, "It is true you killed a deer. I will lead you over to get the medicine and we'll eat when you get back." She led him to the fat and he could see again.

"Don't you taste any till I come back," he begged. "We'll eat together," she said. "Go on, hurry. Take this," and she handed him the fat. "When the water comes up under your arm throw it in, but don't look back at it. Come back without looking back."

Coyote started off, but he looked back and saw the woman cooking. "Don't eat till I come," he called. He had not even gone as far as the shore when he thought, "I didn't even see the medicine she gave me. I had better look at it so I'll know what medicine to use if my eyes become sore again." He saw it was fat. "Why, that's not medicine, that's something to eat," he said and bit it. He had just swallowed it all when everything got black before him. He tried and tried to vomit it up, but in vain, so he began to cry loudly. "What's the matter now?" said the woman. "You crazy Coyote, you'll have rust around your eyes. You are crazy if you think I'll lead you around again soon. You can just keep wandering around by yourself."

She went off in disgust and left Coyote running along crying. He ran into something and felt around, it was a tree. He took some pitch and rubbed it in his eyes. Then he could see a little, but everything looked blurry. He got more pitch, but whenever it got warm the pitch melted and he had to keep on making new eyes.

After a time he saw a house and heard someone singing. An old woman lived there with her four grandchildren who were dancing and singing with Coyote's eyes. The old woman herself was singing while she pounded sunflower seed. Coyote went in and saw she was blind. "Well, you are pounding away," he said cheerfully. She did not answer so he tried again, "I see you are home today." There was no answer so Coyote spoke again, "How are you doing?" "Don't you know anything?" she said suddenly. "No," Coyote answered. "Don't you know Coyote took away my eyes?" "Your granddaughters are dancing with them," Coyote said. "Oh, I didn't know that," she said. "Come in again tonight and they'll stop playing with the eyes then. Come back and as soon as the sun goes down I will be taken over and I will have my eyes for the night." "All right, I'll come," Coyote said.

Then the old woman warned, "You had better go now, the chief will be there, Chief Coyote." "Is he a chief?" asked Coyote. The woman said, "Really, you are pitiful! Of course Coyote is a big chief like the deer with antlers." "Well, I guess I better go then," Coyote said.

Then Coyote took a stick and killed the old woman. He pulled off her dress and while doing so tore his eye a little. He put her dress on and tied up his eye. Then he laid the old woman in the corner and covered her. Then he sat down, pounded and sang, "My grandchildren are playing with Coyote's eyes."

When the children heard him, they laughed and said, "It is Coyote's voice. What is the matter with our grandmother?" So they went in and asked her why she sang like Coyote. "I have been singing all day, that's why I am hoarse." Then they asked, "Why is your eye tied up like that? "Some of these sunflowers flew into it." "Well, go get ready," they said. "I am ready, "I'll go get Coyote's eyes," sang the old woman.

They ate what she had pounded, then went to the dance. The oldest one carried the old woman on her back. She started to run. "Oh my chest hurts, go more quietly," Coyote begged. "No, we're in a hurry!" She had not gone far with her load when she put it down and her sister took it up. Every time Coyote asked one of them to slow up she refused at first, but finally consented. So it went on until all the woman's grandchildren had carried him. When they came in sight of the dance-hall, the youngest put him down and the people helped him in. Coyote said, "Where are Coyote's eyes?" They set the pot of water containing them near him. He felt around in it. "Here are my eyes lying in the water. Oh thank you. At last I have my eyes back. Let's dance now." Coyote took up the eyes and the people began to dance. He sang, "Put out the light. Long ago they used to dance in the dark."

As soon as the light was put out, he tore off the dress and threw it down. Then he spat on the floor and ran out. The spittle kept on singing but it got weaker and weaker. "Let's have light, it sounds like the old woman is dying," someone said. They got a light, but could find no old woman. Instead, they found the spittle singing and the pot with the eyes was empty. Then they said, "It must have been Coyote himself." Outside they heard him laugh. They knew him only too well. "The Chief has taken his eyes from us," they said. Coyote ran off and they chased him.

That's the end of the road.

Story of Lynx

Lynx lived with his grandmother not far from the other people. The chief of the town where Lynx lived had a daughter. One night the people went to the chief's house for a council. Lynx climbed the poles of the chief's house and saw the chief's daughter sleeping. He thought as he looked at her, "Soon she will have a baby." Not long after she had a baby. The chief asked, "Whose child is it?" "I don't know," answered his daughter.

The baby cried all the time. At last the chief said, "If the

83

father would hold his baby it would stop crying." Raven said, "It's my grandchild." "If he stops crying when you take him, it is your child." Raven took the baby but it kept on crying. Coyote said, "Give it to me, it's my grandchild." He took it but it kept on crying. No one could quiet it. Everyone had held it but Lynx who was not there at the time. The chief said, "Go call Lynx."

Lynx told his grandmother, "I must tell you that it's my child and when the people find it out they will kill me. As soon as I take him I will pass him to you. Then you run off with him." So Lynx took his grandmother on his back and sat right near the door. The chief said, "Hand the baby around again and let everyone take him." Each one wanted the child but he would not stop crying. When Lynx took him he stopped crying and laughed. "Let's try once more," ordered the chief, but no one could quiet the child. When it came Lynx's turn again, he let out his claws and clawed the baby, but the baby still stopped crying. The chief said, "We can't allow this. What shall we do to Lynx? Shall we jump on him?"

Lynx threw the baby to his grandmother. Then Coyote took Lynx by the neck, threw him down in the middle of the floor, and they all stamped on him until he sank so far into the ground that only his fur showed. Then the chief said, "Leave him there! Let none of you take pity on my daughter. We will leave her here to die." Everyone left and only the girl and her baby were there. She sat by the fire. Then Magpie turned back. The chief asked, "Where are you going?" Magpie replied, "I forgot something which I need." Magpie went back, took off his blanket, threw it down and cried, "It is for the baby."

Rabbit also pretended he had forgotten something and took his blanket back for the baby. The girl just sat there and cried. She was cold and hungry. Then way off she heard singing, it kept getting nearer and nearer. She found it was Lynx. As he sang his fur began to stand up. He slowly rose out of the ground and got up. He smoothed his body down to his ankles and wrists and up as far as his neck. As he was smoothing his head the girl went and took hold of him. "Don't do that! I am nearly frozen," Lynx said. "You will always think me ugly when you look at me if you don't let me tidy myself." He smoothed his feet until they were smooth and neat. She said, "You're good enough." Lynx replied, "You will look at me and think me ugly." "No, no, you are all right as you are." So he said, "All right, I'll make our house. Let me go." He made a good house and built a fire. He killed game and they always had plenty to eat.

The people who had left made camp and began to hunt. Magpie and Rabbit each killed a fawn but the rest of the men caught nothing. After a time they were all starving. Finally the chief said, "I guess someone had better go and see Lynx." "I'll go," volunteered Coyote.

He went and when he arrived, he saw that there was a fire in the house. The little boy was now big enough to play about. His mother had given him a tallow disk to roll. Coyote watched where it stopped and waited there. When the child rolled it again it stopped near Coyote. He grabbed it with his mouth, but the boy chased him and howled, "He is going to eat my toy." His mother came out and asked, "What is the matter?" "Coyote is trying to eat my toy."

She caught Coyote and choked him. Then she tore the fat out of his mouth and gave it to the boy. When Coyote got back home he said nothing, no matter what the people asked him. Some days afterward Raven said, "I'll take my turn. I'll go to see if we can get something to eat from Lynx." The same thing happened to him. When the woman choked him, his eyes turned white. He lay there for a time, and finally got up and went back, but would answer no questions. "Why are your eyes so white?" "I don't know," he replied.

The next morning Rabbit said to Magpie with whom he lived, "Let us go and see Lynx." They came to Lynx's house and saw many deer sides hanging outside. They wanted to take them, but the woman came out. "Come in," she said. She gave them a lot to eat. "We and all our people are starving," they told her. "Why don't you come here? Come whenever you want to." They ate and ate. "Eat until you have enough," she said. "No, we are saving some for our children." "That is not necessary. Eat until it is all gone. Then you will have something to take back to your children anyhow." They ate it all and said, "We guess we'll go now." She fixed a pack of food for them to take back. "When you get back don't grudge it. Put it all down and let your children eat their fill. Then if there is any left, dry it."

They took the food home. Rabbit's and Magpie's children ate loudly. The people asked, "Why do they make that noise? They never do that at other times. Maybe they are dying and eating each other." Lynx's wife had given Magpie and Rabbit strips of dried fat to take home. This was the choicest food one could offer. The Rabbits were chewing these strips with one side of the mouth and pine moss with the other so that if the people should look in they would not see that they had meat. A person went over and peeped in at the door. "I don't see what it is. Maybe they are choking."

The people went to bed. The next morning Rabbit and Magpie left again. The people said, "They have no fire. Go see what is the matter, maybe they all died." Raven said, "I'll go." He flew over and soon the people heard a noise as if something were being caught. He went in and everything was quiet. He did not come out. After a time the chief said, "Go see. If anyone died, Raven is probably picking out his eyes." The man who peeped in saw that Raven was eating meat. The chief said, "Take it from him and bring it to me." They brought it over. "Come, we'll all have a little."

The people all came to the chief's house. The chief cut the meat into small pieces and each person had a bit. "Now, we'll pay damages to my daughter. We'll take her some presents. Each of you put something in this blanket," ordered the chief. They contributed cloth, handkerchiefs, a big pile of valuables of every kind they had. "Take it to her and say it is from her father. He wants to come back, all his people are starving."

The people took the blanket full of valuables over to Lynx's house. The woman looked at them when they came in and turned away. Lynx tried to be polite. "So you have come here," he said. They put down the bundle. "That is what your father sent you. Now I guess we must go back." No one said a word. Lynx thought, "It's up to the woman. Whatever she thinks will be all right." His wife said nothing. Finally she got up and untied the bundle of presents. "No! I won't accept it! Bluebird's coat of blue is not there," she said. The girl said to her husband,

86

"They are unreasonable to offer me what they don't want themselves."

The people picked up the bundle and took it back to the chief. "Your child said, 'No, I won't accept it. Bluebird's coat is not there.'" "Go call Bluebird," said the chief. The chief sent Bluebird's coat over. The men laid it down. "Here is what you want," they said. She laughed, "Go tell them to come in."

They went in and saw the house full of meat. The people were fed and went home. Coyote came in. "Just bones," he said as he untied the sack he had brought back with him. He untied another and found it full of fat. He ran to the chief and complained, I got nothing but bones and fat." He was told, "I can't help it. Tomorrow we'll get fresh meat." The next day the people led by Lynx went hunting. They shot many deer. Each person caught two and Coyote had two fawns.

That's the end of the story of Lynx.

Dog Husband

Two sisters lived together. The older was the wife of Eagle who was the chief of the village. When she heard that her younger sister had gotten married, she thought, "I'll go see my brother-in-law." She went there and saw her sister sitting with an ugly man. She said to her, "Why did you choose such a homely man? There are plenty of good-looking ones." He was very old and so blind he could not see the people, the Lynxes, Fishers, and everyone. The younger sister said, "Shut up! Go back to your old Eagle. Actually, he has a long crooked nose. That's the kind you chose for your husband." The older girl went home.

Across the river an ermine was seen on a bush. Coyote shouted, "Go set a trap for ermine." All the people went and set traps and watched them, but the ermine ran right through their traps without getting caught. The people came back. Then the younger sister led her husband out to try trapping. When they were seen, someone remarked, "If those handsome young fellows can't catch ermine, how can an old blind man expect to succeed?" The old man said nothing, but he and his wife went past the place where the other traps were set. He set a trap and his wife led him back home, but they had only gone as far as the open country when the ermine began biting at the trap.

Coyote cried out, "What does that old duffer think he is going to do?" The people ran out to take the ermine, but the wife said, "Leave it alone, he is going to use it for his eyes." They gave it to her. The next day the older sister said to her, "What are you going to use that for, the ermine you took from those boys?" The younger sister paid no attention to her, but went in. Night came and then it was morning and the older sister thought, "I'll go and reason with my sister."

She went to her house, but saw her sitting by a handsome man. She did not say a word. The wife was combing his hair and fixing it. Her sister said, "You're hurting him, let me comb him." She came up closer to the man and kept edging closer and closer saying, "Give me that comb. I'll comb him myself." Her sister hit her hands with the comb. "Go to your Eagle! Fix his hair if you want a man." But the older sister sat still. Again she was told, "Go back to your Eagle," and she went back. Soon she came prepared for a long visit. Finally, the wife said to her husband, "Come, let's go back to your people." However, the older sister went along. They came to the home of the husband's relatives and the older sister found out that they were all dogs. She saw her sister sitting in the house with dogs all around her. The younger sister told the older not to come near but to sit far away from them. But she wanted to sit close to them. At night they ate some kind of meat. They all ate, the younger sister, her husband, and all the dogs. Eagle's wife alone did not eat it. Her sister said, "Eat!" She replied, "Why should I eat like a dog?"

A dog lay down beside her and she hit it. "Stop that!" warned her younger sister, but she did not listen to her. At night the dogs, which were all spotted, went to sleep. Eagle's wife sat up and kept hold of a stick with which she hit the dogs. "Lie down and go to sleep!" her sister told her. At last she went to sleep. Then the woman and her husband left her. When she awoke she was crowded upon by dogs. She jumped up and hit them and they ran off. The younger sister was gone and Eagle's wife did not know where to go. She cried and she stayed in the house. At night she slept again and the spotted dogs all came back. She hit at them with a stick, but they crowded her anyway.

When she woke she heard something which sounded like people talking. They were not far off. They were laughing. "My clothes are all worn out because I was beaten, the beads are all broken and lost," said one. Another said, "My necklace is worn because I was beaten so." They laughed again. The third said, "My bracelet is in shreds, she beat me up terribly." "My earrings are ruined," said another and they laughed again. Suddenly they were gone. The girl got up and looked. She saw that they had a fire and men were standing around it. All their clothes, their moccasins and trousers were embroidered in beads. She went in and thought, "They are people, I will not beat them anymore."

She lay down. They went into the sweathouse and by daybreak all was quiet. She thought, "I'll go see what they're doing." Where the men had been standing there were only broken white beads. She went back in and cried. The dogs were gone, but they were people. She stayed there alone and cried. After some time she gave birth to children, but they were dogs. She thought, "I won't leave them, I'll take care of them." She covered them and kept them warm.

In the morning she would go out, travel about and come back. She would feed them and go out again. Once when she went to the fireplace she saw the tracks of little people with those of the puppies. She thought, "Someone must have been here who had a baby."

The next day she went out again. When she came back she saw the baby tracks with those of the puppies. She thought, "Someone must have been here again. Why did that person come with its dog?" She looked at her own pups and saw they were all right. At last she decided to spy on them.

She went into a corner and covered herself with a blanket leaving only a hole just big enough for her eyes. There she kept watch. She heard her dogs say. "It's about time for us to play." One, a little girl, said, "I'll see where our mother is." She went out. Soon she came back and said, "It's all right, she's gone."

The mother saw her lead a little dog around the fire by a rope which was fastened around his neck. She said something to him in her language, then she hit him. As they were running she said it again and he answered. She hit him again. Then their mother jumped up. She took hold of the girl and said, "Stop!" She answered, "No, I'm very lonesome and I'm trying to teach him to be a little person, too." "No! It will be all right this way. He will be our dog, but we will be kind to him." Then the mother lived with her daughter who was a person and her son who was a dog.

That is all I know! That is the end of the trail.

Catbird

Catbird was a little boy who lived with his grandmother. One day he said, "I ought to have something to shoot with." "Impossible!" said his grandmother, "I have no materials to make it." "I'll go look for something," he said.

He walked until he came to a river. Then he called to an elk, "Give me a ride, my father's sister, my father's sister." The elk answered, "No, my flesh is too old and tough and my fat is coarse." Another elk came by, one of the old elk's children. Catbird cried to him, "Give me a ride, my father's sister." The elk answered, "No, I'm too young; my fat is too tender." Then the largest oldest elk was requested to ferry Catbird across. "You are pitiable, come along and sit in the hair of my heel." As he went into the water Catbird cried, "My moccasins are getting wet." "You are pitiable, crawl up to my knee where the hair is longer." Catbird crawled up, then complained, "My moccasins are getting wet." "Come up to the tip of my tail," said Elk.

Catbird went up where the hair was long but still complained. Then he moved up the shoulder and then into Elk's ear, but even there he feared getting wet. "What can we do so you don't get wet?" asked Elk. "Try sitting in the hair of my nose." Catbird went into Elk's nose and did not stop there, but rushed through his nose and throat to his heart. He sat there. "My, it's warm!" he thought. Elk thought, "That rascal of a Catbird! So that was what he went into my nose for."

Catbird took off his little moccasins and hung them up in Elk's heart. Then he did something to the heart and Elk died. Catbird ran out, but he forgot his moccasins. Elk lay on the ground and Catbird sat up high and sang,

"What might I use to sharpen my knife?
What might I use to drop on the whetstone?
tsa---tsar tsar tsar tsar."

A wolf was walking by. He heard Catbird and understood instantly. "He must need a knife," he thought. When Catbird saw Wolf he pretended not to see him. He looked past him and thought, "I suppose he'll take it away from me, my game which lies there." Then he sang,

"How am I going to shave my little arrow?
What may I drop on it to smooth it?
tsa---tsar tsar tsar tsar."

Wolf understood him and asked, "Did you get game?" "No, I made no kill." Wolf said, "But you were just singing.

'How may I sharpen my knife?
What may I drop on my sharpener?' "

"No," said Catbird, "I said,

'How shall I shave it?
How shall I smooth it?' "

They kept arguing in this way until finally Catbird said, "Yes, I got some game." "Where is it?" "It is lying there." Wolf said, "I have a knife, I'll skin it. Go get your mother's brothers so they can come and lick the blood." Catbird said, "I have no moccasins." "Go on, I'll lend you some." "No, they're too big." "I'll fix them for you. I can tie them so they are smaller," said Wolf. Wolf put the moccasins on Catbird and tied them tight. He went out of sight, but only to beat them with a rock until they were in shreds. Then he came back and said to Wolf, "They're all worn out." "What is the matter? They're thick. How did they get all ruined like that? Soon I'll have this elk skinned, then I'll go get your uncles so they will lick your elk's blood."

Wolf ran off and Catbird finished skinning the elk and covered it. Then he ran home to his grandmother. "I got some game but the Wolves will take it from me." "Hurry, take your basket. We'll take it far so they cannot get it." He took his little basket and they ran to where the fresh meat was lying. They put it all in Catbird's basket. They gathered the elkskin. Catbird took off his little shirt and his little hat and hung them on a bush so that it looked just as if he were sitting there himself. They went far away and took the meat to a cliff. Near the edge they smoked the meat. Catbird put five cooking stones into the fire and laid the layer of fat from around the elk's stomach near him.

When Wolf got home he told his four children, "Catbird got an elk, but we'll get it from him. You bite Catbird. When you are biting him, I'll say to you, 'Don't, you'll scare him,' but don't listen to me." They hurried back to the kill and the children ran and growled. Wolf said loudly, "Look out, you'll scare your little nephew." The first ran up to the rotten wood and bit it. Then they sniffed and walked around it. Old Wolf thought, "I wonder why they do not eat it." He came up and the children asked, "Where is the meat?" He uncovered the elk and nothing was there. Then the oldest Wolf said threateningly, "There's no place on earth I do not know."

They looked for tracks and followed them until they saw smoke. The children ran up and saw Catbird. Catbird took a stone from the fire and wrapped the "veil" of fat around it. As the first Wolf came under the edge of the cliff he looked up. Catbird threw down the hot rock with the grease coating and said, "Open your mouth. This will be your first tidbit." He opened his mouth wide and Catbird threw the stone in. Immediately he had heartburn. "Look at your brother," Catbird called. "Why just one bite gives him heartburn!" Then he killed all of the wolves with his five grease-coated rocks.

After Catbird had helped his grandmother smoke the elk meat he prepared sinew for his bow. "I wish I had a bow," he whined. "I wish I could be where the bow-wood tree cracks in the wind." "Impossible!" said his grandmother. "You would probably get caught in the crack yourself." "I'm going to get it anyhow," replied Catbird.

He went anyway. He brought it home and as he sat down to shave it he said, "I wish I had someone to feather my arrow, one who is an expert. I wish Grizzly would do it for me. I think he would do it well." "Impossible!" said his grandmother. "He would bite your head." "You are always saying 'Impossible!' Tomorrow I am going to find out where he is." "He lives right at the edge of the wood in a hole," volunteered the grandmother.

The next morning Catbird went toward the timber and as he approached, he saw Grizzly eating. He said, "Never mind. I won't shoot you, I came to ask you to feather my arrow." "All right," said Grizzly and went back with Catbird. As they came near the house Catbird said, "Wait here. Let me go in." He went in and said to his grandmother, "Why don't you have a fire?" She went out for wood and saw Grizzly standing by the door. She ran in and said to Catbird, "Why do you do such outrageous things?" "Well," said Catbird innocently, "he'll be a great help. He is going to feather my arrow."

In the morning Catbird got the wood for the arrows. As the arrows were being made he said, "I wish I had some eagle feathers." "Impossible!" exclaimed his grandmother. "What would you do with them if you had them?" Catbird said, "I'll go get some." He searched long and finally found an eagle's nest with Eagle's children in it. The mother Eagle was away looking for something for them to eat. She caught Catbird and carried him to the nest and laid him in it alive. When the little eagles ate, he ate, too. I don't know how long he stayed there, he was there until the feathers of the little eagles had grown to just the right size for his purpose. Then he tied two of the eagles together and prodded them until they flew out of the nest and he sat among their feathers. They were not able to fly far but flopped to the ground. He pulled out some wing and tail feathers and went home. He laid the feathers down in front of Grizzly who finished feathering Catbird's arrow. The Catbird sent him away.

One day Catbird was wandering about and suddenly came to the shore of a lake. He sweated for many days. Then he saw a fish in the water. "I wish I had a line and hook." Somehow he got some fishing tackle. He fished and got a bite. "I wish I had a bucket," he went on. He had another bite, pulled in the line and found he had fished up a bucket. He cooked the fish but did not share it with his grandmother. When he went home his grandmother gave him some food but he did not eat. Again he sweated and again he fished. Again he got a bite and cooked and ate the fish all by himself. When his grandmother offered him food he said, "No, I am not hungry." When he had gone off somewhere the grandmother went to the shore to investigate and found his bucket. There were pieces of fish sticking in it and on the bottom was a small fish eye. She was sorry that Catbird was so stingy.

The next morning when he went to sweat she called to him, "I'm leaving you. You didn't share a shred of your fish with me." He looked up and saw his grandmother going up into the air with something on her back. "Don't leave me," he called, "come back to me." "No, I'm leaving you for good, you didn't share a bit with me." In vain he implored her. He cried for a long time, then went to the shore and sweated. Then he fished and everything he wished for appeared on the hook. He fished up a blanket. Then he ran to his mother's father and said, "I can fish up anything I choose to mention, just like that! All I need to do is to fish and wish."

"You think that is good luck? You'll find it is the other way around." Catbird, however, was excited and went back and fished up a knife, a dish and other things. Then, "I wish I had a mate," he said. At that he felt his line begin to pull. He pulled hard and fished out a person. He ran to his mother's father. "I fished out a person." "You had better listen to me. That is all for no good," said his grandfather.

Catbird went back and saw a girl sitting there. Then he said, "I wish I had a child." He threw in his hook and this time fished up a child. He ran to his grandfather and said, "This time I fished up a child." Again his grandfather warned him, "You better watch out. You'll go too far and then you'll die."

Catbird went back to the shore and the girl said to him, "Let's go back to my parents." Once more he ran to his grandfather. "She tells me, "Come back to my people.'" "I've already warned you. You are going to die, but I will go with you. Then at least you will not be alone."

94

They all got into a canoe, Catbird, the girl with the baby, and the grandfather. The whole canoe with its load dived to the bottom of the water. They saw a house on the shore, but the shore itself was all covered with ice. The grandfather went up to it and did not even slip. When he came up to the door he recognized the girl's parents. "Whatever you do to us we'll do to you," he said.

Then Catbird and the girl and the baby came up and they all went in. The house was made of ice and frost. When the child was taken from its mother it disappeared. After they had stayed two days Catbird's grandfather said, "Let's go back." "I am not going back again," said the girl. "Neither am I," said Catbird. "No, let's go back together. They have already eaten your child, they will eat you too. They are man-eating monsters."

So just Catbird and his grandfather went back to the canoes and it came up to the surface of the water again.

Skunk and Fisher

Skunk and Fisher lived together in a place where there were many deer. They would go hunting every morning and would kill two deer. Fisher would clean them and prepare the meat, then Skunk would say, "Don't give me any meat, just the entrails, the fat, and the meat near the back of the tail. That's all I ever want. You just give me those scraps from now on." Customarily they did that. Fisher hunted and secured plenty of meat but Skunk took only the scraps.

Not far from where they lived there was a village. Eagle was the chief there and he had two daughters. The younger was Chipmunk, the elder was Squirrel. One day he said to them, "Go to Fisher so he will give you meat." Before they left, their mother said, "When you go in look carefully at the meat. What Skunk gets is no good, it's only scraps. Fisher gets the only good meat."

So the girls went. They came into the house, sat down, and

looked at the things Skunk had at the head of his bed, then at the things Fisher had. Just as it became dark they heard Skunk's noise. He made this noise every time he took a step. Chipmunk had to laugh at this, but Squirrel, her sister, said, "Keep quiet and come under the mat so he cannot see you." Meanwhile Skunk came nearer and Chipmunk was convulsed with giggles. He heard her and saw them. Then he asked, "Did your parents tell you to come to Fisher's bed? There's my bed." He grabbed one of them by the arm and made her go in behind his pillow. Then the other hid there too. Skunk set about making a fire, but soon they heard a new noise. It was Fisher. Then Squirrel said to her sister, "Didn't I tell you! What a nice noise he has!"

Fisher laid down two deer and said to Skunk, "Come, drag them in!" Skunk said, "You make me ashamed. What if someone heard you say that?" Fisher thought, "That's funny! He never said that before." Skunk dragged in the deer and as Fisher cut them up he said, "Give me some of the ribs to cook." Fisher thought, "I won't be stingy. I'll give him some."

He prepared the meat, gave some to Skunk and they both cooked. When the food was done and they were ready to eat Skunk said, "Let's share with our pillows." "What do we want to feed our pillows for?" asked Fisher. "It's all right," said Skunk. He took a dish, put meat in it and set it just behind his pillow. Then he watched it while he and Fisher ate. When they had finished Skunk said, "Let's look." His plate was the same, so he told Fisher to look at his. "What do I want to do that for?" "Oh, go ahead." Fisher looked and the plate was empty, only bones were left.

"My, there must be someone here," said Skunk. Fisher thought, "I wonder why he says that. He never said it at other times."

At night they went to bed. Fisher laid a stick on the fire, but Skunk said, "You are making it too hot for me." Fisher replied, "No, I feel sore, my back hurts." They both lay near the fire. As the fire died down, the house became dark and Skunk got up. Just as he got near his pillow Fisher kicked the wood and it lighted up the house. So Skunk came back and lay down. Fisher kept it light this way all night.

In the morning they got up and cooked. Again as they were dishing up the food Skunk said, "Let us share with our pillows." Fisher protested but again they put food near the pillows. When they had finished eating they looked at the dishes they had put near their pillows. When they finished Skunk's was the same as before, but on Fisher's plate there were only bones.

Fisher then went out and rolled a disk which make a noise like a bullroarer. Skunk thought, "He's gone now," but Fisher had gone out only to hide near the house in the brush. Then Skunk said to the girls, "Come with me, Fisher is already gone." So Squirrel and Chipmunk went with him. He ran around making his noise. Chipmunk always laughed when he did that, but Squirrel was quiet. Soon Skunk said, "Go back into the house. I am going away, too." Fisher saw him go and when Skunk got out of sight Fisher went into Skunk's bed where the two girls were hiding. "What are you doing here? Did your people tell you 'Go to Skunk's?' What were you going to get from him? Look at what I gave him, nothing but disgusting odds and ends." Squirrel said, "Chipmunk laughs too much." Fisher said, "Go over there. We'll leave Skunk and take the meat supply along." They took the food and burned the house. It made a lot of smoke, but they went around the smoke and left.

Meanwhile Skunk had been eating grass. When he had eaten enough he lay down on his back. He saw the smoke and thought, "The Cayuse must be burning the Coeur d'Alene." Then he noticed that the smoke was near and he got up and ran. As he came closer he saw it was near his own house. As he went over the hill he was sure of it. "Oh, the chief's daughters, they may have died," he cried. He ran as fast as he could, but when he got there the house was burned. "The Squirrels died," he cried. He took a stick and stirred the fire thinking, "I might find some bones." But he did not find any. Then he wondered, "What could have become of them?" He sat down and thought, "I'll leave. Maybe Fisher will come back at night and then we'll find out what happened to the Squirrels." However, Fisher did not come back at night. Then Skunk thought, "I will go over the earth to find them. There is no corner where I will not go."

97

So he started off. When he had gone far he found tracks of three people, Fisher's between the tracks of the Squirrel girls. He followed their tracks for a time but became thirsty. He saw a cliff and underneath it a spring and went to drink. When he got to the water he saw the Fisher party deep in the water. "You are going to die," said Skunk, "leave Squirrel and Chipmunk." But Fisher only laughed at him and did not go away. "All right! You'll all die." So saying he sprayed his fluid there in the water. They laughed, so he did it again until he had no more. His strength had all gone into the water. He ate again and when he had enough he went back to the water. He lay down and thought, "I'll do that lying down this time." He lay on his back and looked up at the top of the cliff where he saw the three were sitting. He got up and said to the girls, "Leave him! I am going to squirt my fluid into his eyes." They said nothing, but laughed. Then Fisher said to them, "Go far away. He can't reach me anyway." The girls went far away and then Skunk sent his fluid into Fisher's eyes. Skunk said to the Squirrel girls, "Jump down," but the girls paid no attention. "Hurry!" Skunk repeated, "If you don't come down I'll do the same thing to you."

They came down and said they were sorry. Skunk said to them, "What business had you to go with Fisher?" So they went away with Skunk. At night Skunk ordered them to fix his bed and the poor girls were obliged to do it. They chose a smooth spot, piled grass high for a mattress and then Skunk lay down. He said, "You, Squirrel, will be my pillow." The poor thing lay down. "You, Chipmunk, get under the calf of my leg for a support." She had to get under his leg. In the morning Skunk was asleep when Chipmunk woke up. She said to her sister, "Wake up!" Squirrel answered, "I am already awake. Go get a piece of wood. Put it down here where I am." As her sister put it down she crawled out from under Skunk's head. They put a piece of wood under his legs. Then they ran off.

Skunk kept on sleeping. He finally woke up and said, "Chipmunk, wake up! You have no flesh, you are hard." Then he threw back his head and called Squirrel, but no, she was not there! There was nothing but a stick of wood. "Now you are going to get it!" he threatened when he found that neither of the girls was there. He ran off, found their tracks and followed them. He came to a place where camas was being baked in a pit. Someone said to him, "Maybe you are Skunk." Skunk said, "I'm hungry for cooked camas."

The pit was just being uncovered and the food was taken out. Skunk sat at some distance even though the people asked him to sit nearer. "No, just pass a dish over to me here," he said. He took a sack, dumped the camas on it, and ate. He tied some camas up for his lunch and got up to go. Where he had been sitting the people saw some camas which had been spilled. "Look, you spilled some," they told him. "No, I tied it up and fastened it to my belt," he said. Then they asked, "Are you leaving it?" "No, I've already eaten the camas," he said.

Again Skunk came to a settlement. Again he did not sit with the people but sat a little apart. At night someone cried and the chief said, "Go see the baby." It was dark so Skunk went. He saw there were many houses. He peeped in and saw all the people passing a baby around from one to the other. He was not seen, so he cupped his two hands, moved among the people, and took the baby. The people said, "Where is it? It is gone!" Then they scattered.

In the morning they saw Skunk who said to them, "I have something to tell you." The chief called the people together. "Come we have something to announce!" Skunk said, "Sit down. I want to tell you. I just came from Cayuse country. As I passed by the enemy ran after me. There must have been a hundred of them. I did my best but my first-born was captured. I came on but a hundred and fifty of the enemy attacked me. My second-born was captured. I kept on running. I crossed the river in the Cayuse country. Then my third child was captured. I'll stop right here. I want to go out."

He got up and just as he got to the door they could see his fists were apart and he was holding something in them. He squirted his fluid on the door poles and the people all fell back. The Skunk was gone. On the way Skunk had thrown his fluid on Antelope right near the tail. He threw some on the little animals which became wild canaries. That is why their feathers are yellow. Fox ran out, but Skunk saw Coyote. All the people died.

Two poor old blind women were standing at the door. "How are you?" said Skunk. One old woman pointed to her left eye, "I can see just a little." Skunk sent some fluid in the eye and she could see. Then he threw some into the eye of the other blind woman. "Fine! I can see everything now," she said. "I've got my eyes back again." Then Skunk asked the old women, "Are there many people over here?" "Yes," they said. "Carry me back to pay me for curing you," he said.

They said, "We'll take you in a canoe." Skunk said to them, "You must respect me as if I were a chief." He sat in the canoe in state. One of the old women sat in front of him, the other behind. As they moved on, one old woman said, "There is a nice village; it is white with houses." Skunk said, "Call out! Say, 'Here comes a chief with yellow moccasins. He has stripes at the back of his head and on his back. His eyes and his tail are striped.' "

The people crowded out to shore, while Skunk sat very dignified with his arms folded as if he were a chief. The chief and his people lifted him by the arms and carried him up to the village. So they went. They made the noise of transformation and became stars.

This is the end of this road.

Thunder

Once there was a man who would go away in the daytime and come back in the evening. His wife was visited by Thunder when he was gone. One day Thunder said, "I'm coming for you and you will go away with me." In the evening the husband came back and his wife was gone. He sat down and thought, "I wonder where she went."

After I don't know how many days he thought, "I'll go look for my wife." He went far away. After a long time he came to a house and went in. The people there asked, "Ah! Are you looking for your wife?" "Yes." "You poor thing! You'll never see her again. Thunder took her." "I'm going to continue to search for her," he replied. The owner of the house gave him four small needles. "Go in that direction," he commanded and the man went. He came to a house and went in. "Are you looking for your wife?" he was asked. "Yes." "You are to be pitied, you'll never see her again." "All right! But, I will look for her." This one also gave him four needles and told the man, "My older brother will point it out to you." He went on. He came to a house and the same conversation was held. Again he was given four needles. A fourth time it happened. "Thunder has your wife. You'll never see her," he was warned. "They gave you those things for nothing, but go on. Not far from here you'll see a high cliff. Use the needles there. If you can climb to the top you might see your wife, but you will never get there."

He went on until he came to the cliff. He took out a needle and stuck it into the rock. He took out another and stuck it in, and thus with a third and a fourth. Then they were all used and he saw no woman. There was nothing against the rock, but soon Chipmunk came into sight, leaping up the cliff. "Please help me get to my goal," begged the man. "Take me to the top. Have pity on me, my fingernails are all worn down to the flesh." She said, "Hold on to my tail." He held on to her tail and she leaped up, but they had not gone far when she complained of her fingernails. The man took out a needle and Chipmunk ran away.

Soon he saw someone else against the rock. It was Squirrel leaping along. "Squirrel," he begged, "take pity on me. See how my fingernails are worn down." "Take hold of my tail," she replied. He took her tail and she leaped among the rocks. However, she had not gone far before she said, "My fingernails are worn close." He took out a needle and begged piteously. This time Squirrel came leaping and told him to hold her tail. They climbed until she was worn out, so he took out a needle and hung back.

Soon Feathers came. He said to them, "Help me!" "You should have asked me long ago. Take hold of me." He took hold. They were blown to the rock and touched it. Then they were blown away again. Four times they blew out and back. Then they were at the top and the Feathers said, "Go! You can

101

climb the rest alone. The one who is up there is not a person and he will kill you. You see all the trees are broken from lightning. That is because he goes hunting and when he returns at night and comes into the house lightning hits the trees. The woman is there. He takes her by the arms and throws her aside and says, 'Your husband is on earth.' Then he digs and digs in vain. At last he will be quiet. All right then. Go! You may see your wife."

He went far and everywhere he saw splintered trees and rocks broken in two. At last he came to a house. He went in and saw his wife sitting there. He said, "You are dead, you are no longer a person." She said, "Sit down, eat well. If you die it will be good. It is easy to know when he is coming and the food is ready for him." He finished eating. Then the woman said, "We'll make a hole under the bed and you sit in the hole. If he says, 'There is someone in the hole,' and throws me aside and digs, just keep still. After his excitement he will quiet down. Then I'll cook and we'll eat. Then he'll talk nicely. He'll laugh and tell me stories. At night we'll sleep. I'll tell stories, then I'll talk and laugh until he is asleep. I'll tickle him to prove he is fast asleep. Then I'll dig you out. You come out and we'll go away."

Just as Thunder was going to sleep the woman tickled him, but he was snoring, so she jumped up and dug her husband out. She said to him, "When he goes to bed he hangs up his shirt." All the old shirts were hanging on the wall and the woman took all of them along. She threw away the old ones saying, "They are all torn."

They ran to the edge of the cliff and the woman put on the good shirt. They flew back to the earth. She took off the shirt and told it, "Be torn in pieces," then she threw it away and they went to their house.

Meanwhile, Thunder slept. When he woke, the woman was gone. He got up and saw the hole and said, "There's no place I don't know. I will find you and will kill you." He went to get his shirt, but it was gone. The old ones were gone as well as the new one. He sat down and cried.

That's the end.

Nez Perce Myths

Mosquito and Coyote

Mosquito and his grandmother were living together and Mosquito bit his grandmother to death and sucked all of her blood. Then he ate all of her body. He then built a canoe and drifted downstream in it. He bawled and he wept as he went along, lamenting the death of his grandmother. "Oh, my grandmother, oh, my grandmother, oh, my grandmother, oh, my grandmother," he kept saying as he went along. Then Coyote dashed out to the bank of the river toward him and said, "Why is it, Mosquito, that you weep so much?" Mosquito replied, "It is only because I went hunting and shot an antlered buck which I brought home. My grandmother ate the fat but it happened that the fat was rotted and she died of the poisonous fat."

Coyote now began to suspect him and accordingly said to him, "Put into shore for roots." Mosquito answered, "That is just exactly what I dislike, that is just exactly what I dislike. Oh, my grandmother, oh, my grandmother." Coyote said to him again, "Put into shore for root-loaf." "That is particularly distasteful to me, that is particularly distasteful to me. Oh, my grandmother, oh, my grandmother." Here Coyote turned to the people and said, "Make your noses bleed. It is very likely that he has killed his grandmother." They made their noses bleed, and bled five pails full. Now Coyote said to Mosquito, "Put into shore for five pails of blood are full." Mosquito replied quickly to that, "Can't be true, can't be true, can't be true, can't be true." Mosquito was so eager to put into shore that he broke a paddle, but he seized it quickly. He put into shore speedily saying as he went, "Can't be true, can't be true, can't be true, can't be true."

He arrived at the shore and Coyote said to him, "So it was so piteously that my grandfather's brother's daughter came to her end?" "Yes, that is what happened." "Then tie your canoe here," Coyote told him. Mosquito tied his canoe there and they went to the lodge. Coyote said to him, "There is your blood, five pails full. Eat just as much as you like. I shall be busy outside."

Coyote went outside and there he burned off the rye grass leaving it a stubble. Now Mosquito dipped his head into one pail entirely draining it, then into another he dipped his head, draining it entirely, then into another and another until he drained them all but the last. His belly now became taut. He dipped his head into the fifth and drained half. Now his belly became stretched tight and protruded on all sides.

Coyote then shouted to him from outside, "Your canoe is floating away, your canoe is floating away." Mosquito jumped to his feet and dashed from the lodge. His belly was very large but he ran down the hill. There he stumbled and fell. He popped open and gush! He bled to death, because Coyote had burned the grass to a stubble which was like so many needles. Coyote said to the dead one, "Where could you have been hunting that she would have died from rotten fat? You, yourself, bit your grandmother to death. The human race is coming only a short time away and they will say, 'It is already this time of the year, for the mosquito is buzzing.' "

Coyote and Monster

Coyote was building a fish-ladder, by tearing down the waterfall at Celilo, so that salmon could go upstream for the people to catch. He was busily engaged at this when someone shouted to him, "Why are you bothering with that? All the people are gone, the monster has killed them." "Well, said Coyote to himself, "then I'll stop doing this, because I was doing it for the people, and now I'll go along too."

From there he went along upstream by the way of the Salmon River country. Going along he stepped on the leg of Meadowlark and broke it. Meadowlark shouted in a temper, "You have no chance of finding the people if you go along like that." Coyote then said, "My aunt! Please tell me where they are and afterwards I will make you a leg of brush-wood." So

Meadowlark told him, "The people have already been swallowed by a monster." Coyote then replied, "Well, then that is where I am going."

From there he travelled on. Along the way he took a good bath saying to himself, "I don't want to taste repulsive to him." Then he dressed himself all up, "So he won't vomit me up or spit me out." Finally, he tied himself with rope to three mountains, and from there he came up and over many ridges. Suddenly, he saw a great head. He quickly hid himself in the grass and gazed at it. Never before in his life had he seen anything like it. It was such a large thing that its gigantic body melted away off somewhere into the horizon. Then Coyote shouted to him, "Oh monster, we are going to inhale each other!" The big eyes of the monster roved around looking all over for Coyote but did not find him because Coyote's body was painted with clay and blended perfectly with the grass.

Coyote had on his back a pack consisting of five stone knives, some pure pitch, and a flint firemaking set. Presently Coyote shook the grass to and fro and shouted again, "Monster! We are going to inhale each other." Suddenly the monster saw the swaying grass and replied, "Oh, Coyote, you swallow me first, you inhale first." Now Coyote tried. Powerfully and noisily he drew in his breath and the great monster swayed and quivered.

Then Coyote said, "Now you inhale me, for you have already swallowed all the people, so swallow me, too, so I become lonely." Now the monster inhaled like a mighty wind. He carried Coyote along, but as Coyote went he left along the way great camas roots and great serviceberries, saying, "Here the people will find them and will be glad, for the coming of the human race is only a short time away." He almost got caught on one of the ropes but he quickly cut it with his knife, and was pulled right into the monster's mouth.

From there Coyote walked along down the throat of the monster. Along the way he saw bones scattered about and he thought to himself, "It is easy to see many people have been dying." As he went along he saw some boys and he said to them, "Where is his heart? Come along and show me!" However, as they were all going along, Bear rushed out

107

furiously at him. "So!" Coyote said to him, "You make yourself ferocious only to me," and he kicked Bear on the nose. As they were going along Rattlesnake bristled at him in fury. "So! You are vicious only to me." Then he kicked Rattlesnake on the head and flattened it out for him. Going on he met Brown Bear who greeted him, "I see that the monster selected you for the last." Coyote answered, "So! I'd like to save your people." All along the people hailed him and stopped him in this way.

Finally, Coyote told the boys, "Pick some wood up." Here his friend Fox hailed him from the side, "The monster is such a dangerous fellow, what can you do to him?" "So!" replied Coyote. "You, too, hurry along and look for wood." Presently Coyote arrived at the heart and he cut off slabs of fat and threw them to the people. "Imagine you being hungry under such conditions, and grease your mouths with this." And now Coyote started a fire with his flint, and shortly smoke drifted up through the monster's nose, ears, eyes, and anus.

Now the monster said, "Oh, you Coyote, that's why I was afraid of you. Oh, you Coyote, let me cast you out." And Coyote replied, "Yes, and later let it be said, 'He who was cast out is officiating in the distribution of salmon.' " "Well, then, go out through the nose." Coyote replied, "And will not they say the same?" And the monster said, "Well, then, go out through the ears," to which Coyote replied, "And let it be said, 'Here is ear-wax officiating in the distribution of food.' " "Oh, you Coyote! This is why I feared you. Then go out through the anus." But Coyote replied, "And let people say, 'Faeces are officiating in the distribution of food.' "

There was a fire still burning near the heart and now the monster began to writhe in pain, so Coyote began cutting away on the heart, whereupon very shortly he broke the stone knife. Immediately he took another and in a short time this one also broke, and Coyote said to all the people, "Gather up all the bones and carry them to the eyes, ears, mouth, and anus. Pile them up and when he falls dead, kick all the bones outside." Then again with another knife he began cutting away at the heart. The third knife broke and finally the fourth, then only one was left. Then he told the people, "All right, get yourselves ready because as soon as he falls dead, each one will go out of the most convenient opening. Take the old women and old men close to the openings so that they may get out easily."

Now the heart hung by only a very small piece of muscle and Coyote was cutting away on it with his last stone knife. The monster's heart was still barely hanging when Coyote's last knife broke, whereupon he threw himself on the heart and hung on just barely tearing it loose with his hands. In his death convulsions the monster opened all the openings to his body and the people kicked the bones outside and went on out. Coyote, too, went out.

Then the monster fell dead and the anus began to close. But there was Muskrat still inside. Just as the anus closed he squeezed out, barely getting his body through, but his tail was caught. He managed to pull it out, but all the hair was pulled off and it was bare. Coyote just scolded him, "Now always behind in everything." Then he told the people, "Gather up all the bones and arrange them well." They did this, whereupon Coyote added, "Now we are going to carve the monster."

Coyote then smeared blood on his hands, sprinkled this blood on the bones, and suddenly all those who had died while inside the monster came to life again. They carved the great monster and now Coyote began throwing out portions of the body to various parts of the country — toward the sunrise, toward the sunset, toward the warmth, toward the cold. Each part of the body became the people in that place — Coeur d'Alene, Cayuse, Pend d'Oreilles, Flathead, Blackfeet, Crow, or whoever came to live there. He used the entire body of the monster in this distribution to various lands far and wide. Nothing more remained of the great monster.

And now Fox came up and said to Coyote, "What is the meaning of this, Coyote? You have distributed all of the body to far away lands but have given yourself nothing for this immediate locality." "Well," snorted Coyote, "why didn't you tell me that a while ago before it was too late? I was so engrossed I wasn't thinking. You should have told me that in the first place." And he turned to the people and said, "Bring me some water with which to wash my hands." They brought water and he washed his hands and sprinkled the local regions saying, "You may be little people but you will be powerful.

Even though you will be little people, you will be very, very many. The coming of the human race is only a short time away."

The Glutton

A man always cheated his wife of food. He would shoot game, such as grouse, but he would eat everything on the spot and never bring anything home. His wife, on the other hand, would go to dig roots, peel them, and make up a mush which both of them would eat. The woman finally said to him, "So much eating of roots has given us a craving for meat. Why is it that you never shoot anything?"

One day the woman thought, "I will hide myself today and watch him. Why doesn't he ever shoot anything?" On that morning the woman left him as usual, but hid while her husband was lounging inside. The woman concealed herself and presently she saw him come out carrying a quiver with his sheathed arrows in it. He came on out and looked all around in various directions. The woman said to herself, "The poor fellow is going hunting now."

There were usually many grouse around and as the man walked down the hill, he saw a grouse in a tree and he shot it with great accuracy. The woman thought, "I am thankful that we will each eat half." Then he shot another. "We will eat one apiece," she rejoiced. Again he shot one, then another. The woman counted four in all. "Surely now we will have two apiece," she thought, so she went to dig roots and dug a large amount of camas.

She thought only of eating because she craved meat so strongly and because she knew now that he had shot four grouse. She dug a large amount of roots which she packed home happily and arrived at the lodge to find the man just lounging about. She sat down and waited hopefully for him to tell her of the grouse, but the man said, "Now then, my wife, quickly peel the roots, then grind and mash them." She slowly peeled the camas roots and ground them, thinking. "So he cheats me by not sharing food, probably he does this all the time." Then she made a mush and set it before him and he ate it at once. "No wonder he always eats so heartily. He has been doing this all along." And now the woman had a bad thought, "Tomorrow I will do the same again," she plotted.

In the morning she prepared to go and then hid herself as she had done before. Again the man came out, but this time he seemed somewhat suspicious and alarmed. He looked around carefully and he went down the hill. The woman waited until he was gone and then ran back inside the lodge. She searched for a cache and finally found a large storage excavation which he had dug beneath the bed where he had thrown away all of the feathers, bones, and food scraps. Oh, what a pile of these things were there. Her thoughts by this time were very unkind. She scattered every bit of that which was in the storage excavation all about the lodge and even outside. Then she packed up all her personal things and went away.

In the meantime, the man shot some grouse and he took these home. He found some feathers as he went along. "Oh, oh, feathers. She might find out about me." He picked up the feathers only to find more further along. "Where do the feathers come from?" he thought. He picked up more feathers as he went along all the way to the lodge and saw even more feathers as he came to the lodge. "Who has found me out?" he thought. Then, he noted the absence of her personal things. He spent several days at the lodge thereafter, but he felt lonely and sad. Then he decided, "I will go where the people are gathered," so he went. He packed the same quiver and went.

The people were all having a good time. The woman was with them and had no intentions of going back to her husband. The people were dancing with the woman who was surrounded by men. The husband arriving and seeing this became very angry with her. He took an arrow, drew back his bow and aimed at her as she passed by. The people said, "Your husband is about to shoot you." She turned, and saw him standing with drawn bow. She sang, "I am not a grouse, why shoot me?" Suddenly her talk shamed him. His bow fell and he did not shoot her. This poor but not pitiable man went home ashamed and the woman stayed where she was.

Sea Monster Boy

Sea-Monster Boy from the down river people heard that Young Coyote was the best one at hoop spearing. Sea-Monster Boy then contested Young Coyote in spear throwing and Young Coyote defeated him. Sea-Monster Boy's sister was the hoop target which they were spearing and after the contest Sea-Monster Boy said, "Young Coyote, you have defeated me and now I give you my sister." Sea-Monster Boy then went home. Young Coyote now had a wife. Then Young Coyote, his wife, Old Coyote, and Fox all moved to the mountains. There they shot much game which they prepared by drying. In the meanwhile, a baby was born to them.

Old Coyote was making a spoon. "With this I will eat huckleberries and bitterroots at the Wedding Journey feast." Fox was making pure pitch, a pipe, and a spearhead. Old Coyote was thinking only of eating and that is why he made just a spoon. They moved back from the mountains and said to one another, "We are now going on the Wedding Journey." They brought all the meat and many other things for gifts which they packed in a canoe made of a pine tree trunk. Then they embarked downstream.

Sea-Monster Woman sat in the bow and Fox, Old Coyote, and Young Coyote with his son sat in the bottom. In this way they proceeded to the lower reaches of the river. They were going along when they saw the woman in the bow start shoving herself into a dive. Just before they submerged Fox said to them, "Hurry, let us get into the pipe," and all four of them got in and shut the door. The canoe travelled along the water and Sea-Monster Woman thought, "They will be drowned." They were under water a long time and the woman thought, "They are surely drowned by now." They finally rose to the surface again and she saw them dancing their grandson about. "What have they done? I thought they would be suffocated by now," she said to herself. She did the same thing again farther downstream but in no way could she drown them.

112

At last she took them to their destination far down the river and there she said to them, "We have arrived now," and they drifted ashore. The woman was the first to disembark, and immediately she left them and went home. They unloaded their goods, built a fire on the lowlands by the river side, and cooked whatever food they could find.

In the evening the woman came back to them and said, "Here you are. Here is a spear. Something always swims here in the evening. I don't know if it is a person or not, but you must spear it with this. That is what my people said." But she was lying to them. She wanted only to kill them, and when she had gone home before, she had said to her people, "They are powerful. I have wanted to destroy them for sometime, but I could not do it." And then they told her, "Take this old, worn spearhead to them and father will kill all of them when he swims by."

So the woman gave them the spearhead saying, "He comes in the evening, be sure you kill him." Before going she gave them what appeared to be pure pitch but it was really false pitch which is worthless for burning. The woman left them and evening came. Presently they heard him coming and they lighted their torches to watch him coming. Just like a huge person he came along in the water, crawling and grabbling about aimlessly. To all appearances he was a person, and they knew he was Sea-Monster. He came close by and Young Coyote took up Fox's sharp spearhead and at very close range speared the monster under the arm-pit. The monster struggled, but Young Coyote finally managed to kill him.

In the morning the woman came to them again and said, "Well, how did it go? Did the monster swim by last night?" "Yes, and we killed him," they replied. They had hidden their own spearhead and now they showed her the one she had given them. They had covered it with blood, so she would think they had used it. The woman then took the dead monster and said to them as she left, "A monster will come to you again. You must spear it." They had already killed her father and now she was referring to her father's sister's husband. But there sat Coyote unhappily holding his spoon, not having eaten at all.

In the morning the woman came to them and said, "A monster will come again to you." Fox said to his friends, "We have already killed two of them, and now she herself will come. She will come upon us in vengeance, and since she is very ferocious, she is likely to kill us." That evening, Young Coyote's wife came and she was a great gruesome thing. They saw her coming, and so they lighted their torches to show their strength. Should their torches go out, at that moment the sea monster would take them all under water. For that reason they held their torches high and sang even louder, "It is glowing, it is glowing, it is glowing, it is glowing." Young Coyote's son also sang increasingly loud.

They saw her coming and Young Coyote recognized her at once. "It is my wife, all right." She was crawling along, her hair straggling this way and that. Young Coyote speared her, hitting perfectly, but she struggled about very fiercely and then she turned on them. The boy was still singing loudly, "It is glowing, it is glowing."

Then in the midst of the struggle Young Coyote said to them, "Now hurry, go ashore, flee, for she will kill us." Even though he had speared her well she attacked them ferociously, and as they fled the water rose and pursued them in torrents. They ran on as the water surged to their knees. Young Coyote shouted to them, "Now she will kill us, she will carry us under. Release the boy, it is because of him that she is doing this to us." Coyote and Fox were holding the boy by the hand as they ran and Young Coyote again shouted to them, "She is taking us under, release the boy quickly." They let go of the boy there, and immediately the water receded and the flood which had pursued them ceased. Thus Sea-Monster Woman took the child away from them and never again did they see her.

They started home sadly. Somewhere in the flood Coyote's spoon was lost.

The Bears Coyote Killed

Coyote asked, "What are the people doing? Are they hunting buffalo?" They replied, "Yes, hunting buffalo, but Bear takes our kill from us if he learns from the young bears that someone has killed a fat one." "He is certainly a brazen one!" said Coyote.

Now they had another round-up of buffalo, in which Coyote participated, and he killed an exceptionally fat buffalo. They said to him, "Why have you killed such a fat one? Bear will take it from you, he is very frightening." Coyote told them, "I, too, happen to be fierce. Why should you be afraid of him? His ferocity is created only by your talk."

Coyote then began to dress his buffalo. When the people saw the young bears coming, they shouted, "Here come the young bears," and they fled. Even the mice fled. Coyote shouted, "Come here! Why do you run away when you are unafraid of me? Come and hold this beef for me." The young bears, by this time, dashed up to him and said to one another, "Oh, our uncle has a very fat one!" With that they began to snap, bite, and tear at Coyote's kill. Coyote said to them angrily, "Get yourselves away from here," and struck one of the cubs on the nose with his knife. The young bear staggered off to the side and dropped dead.

"What is this that Coyote does? He strikes the young bear dead," the people said to one another. Then they told Bear, "Coyote has struck your child dead." Bear became deeply angry. "Now I'm going to kill Coyote! Why did he ever come! I'm going to kill him now." He dressed himself in full regalia and went forth. Meanwhile, Coyote started a fire and placed two stones to heat. All the people gathered to watch Coyote. They knew Bear was coming because the mice were going about very frightened. "He will kill Coyote," the people said. Then Fox told them, "No, Coyote is the one to be feared. Presently he and I will eat heartily of bear meat."

Then Bear stormed along, bent upon revenge, saying to himself, "Coyote, you are a brazen fellow, but I'll not spare you whatever you may have to say to me." The people saw him coming and they shouted, "Here he comes!" Coyote kept on cutting his buffalo while the others just scattered. "Why do you run away? Hurry and assist me! Hold this for me to carve!" he shouted to the mice. As he cut up the buffalo, Coyote took out the lacey stomach fat and put it aside. Then he took a hot stone out of the fire. He watched Bear come closer. Then he wrapped the hot stone in the lacey fat and, as Bear came right up close, said to him, "Cousin, wait there! Let me toss a bit of fat into your mouth so my fur won't make you vomit."

Bear came to a sudden stop and stood there puzzled. He opened his mouth and Coyote threw the stone in. The hot stone went clear down inside. Bear went into convulsions, turned around, and dashed away. Coyote shouted after him, "Go back to your royal cave!" When Bear got to his cave it began to sizzle from the heat. Coyote shouted to him again, "Go to your royal swimming hole!" Bear jumped into the swimming hole, but the water just boiled. Then Coyote shouted to him again, "Go to your royal dance grounds!" This advice didn't help Bear either because the stone kept burning him. Then Bear fell dead.

"Coyote has killed him already," the people said. "Well, didn't I tell you?" Fox spoke up. "My brother and I will eat well." But they said, "Wait, the Bear's woman will kill Coyote without fail." Fox said, "Impossible! Even the terrible Bear failed to do it." Now the woman charged upon Coyote, after having been told that he had killed her husband. Coyote kept working on his buffalo. He still had one stone in the fire. The people began to shout, "The woman is coming!" Coyote rolled the hot stone in fat and just as she dashed up to him he said to her, "My cousin's wife, wait! Let me toss fat into your mouth so that you will not vomit because of my fur." She, too, stopped and opened her mouth. He threw the fat down her throat and she, too, started to run away. Coyote shouted after her, "Go to your royal cave!" The Bear's cave just sizzled from the heat. Again Coyote shouted to her, "Go to your royal swimming hole!" She went there, but the water just boiled. From there

Coyote said to her, "Go to your royal dance grounds!" She even went there, but it was no use. There she fell dead.

"He has already killed the woman, too," the people said in amazement. Then they all dashed off to ransack Bear's lodge for booty. "No!" Coyote told them, "All of this is mine just as it stands. My elder cousin used to say to me, 'If anything should happen to me everything shall become yours!' Thus my elder cousin used to say to me." Then Coyote moved in and he took in the mice with him. They lived there together.

Skunk White and Eagle

Skunk and Eagle lived together. Skunk always addressed Eagle as brother. Eagle was the hunter and Skunk the preparer of food. Eagle had always said to Skunk, "Never, for any reason, must you come over to my bed because you will make it smell." And Skunk would always reply calmly, "Yes, brother. Why should I want to cross over to your side of the lodge?" Skunk would walk about making his usual noise.

Now there were five sisters, the Killdeer, living nearby. "Let us go and marry Eagle," they planned. The five Frog sisters also decided, "Now we are going to marry Skunk." So they went and all of them arrived at the same time. Skunk was home alone because Eagle had already gone hunting. "We have come to stay permanently," they told Skunk. "We five Killdeer are to stay with Eagle." "And we," the Frogs said, "are to stay with you." But now Skunk objected, "No, you will not do this. You Frogs are ugly and therefore you may not stay with me. Stay over there at Eagle's bed." Skunk then went over and took the Killdeer sisters to his own side of the lodge and put them under his pillow. The Frogs hid themselves under Eagle's pillow.

In the evening Eagle came home and asked, "What have you been doing, Skunk: Why did you come across to my bed?" "Oh, brother, today I had too large a fire and it began to spread over toward your bed and I ran over there to extinguish it. I thought, 'It will not be right for me to burn my brother's bed.'"

117

Eagle answered, "Is that so? You did what you had to, then. I was thinking that you came over here for no reason at all." Then they ate supper. Every few moments Skunk would glance back toward his pillow where he had the Killdeer sisters hidden.

They went to bed after they had finished eating, but soon Skunk began to laugh and laugh. Eagle became angry at last, "You are very annoying, and you are keeping me awake. What are you laughing about?" "Oh, brother," Skunk answered, "It is only that some mice are running on me and it tickles." Right then the Frog sisters whispered to Eagle, "Nephew, let us tell you something. Skunk has the Killdeer sisters under his pillow. They were coming here to you and we were coming to him, but he forbade it and sent us over here to your bed. Then he came over and took the Killdeer sisters over to his bed. He lied to you about the fire. He has the Killdeer sisters under his pillow now and that is why he is laughing." "It is well that you have told me. So this is what he is doing," said Eagle. "Tomorrow when you go home you can take with you all the venison you can carry."

Early the next morning Eagle got up, but Skunk was still asleep. "Why are you sleeping so late!" he scolded Skunk. "Oh, I must have fallen into a profound sleep. That mouse last night kept me awake such a long while," Skunk explained. Eagle went out hunting again, and meanwhile the Frogs packed up a supply of meat and returned home. However, Skunk passed the day there with his wives. Eagle was deeply worried. "What is he trying to do? I will get revenge." That evening when Eagle returned from hunting he said to Skunk, "Skunk, tomorrow you will go with me." Skunk began to complain, "No, brother, I am no hunter. There is nothing I could do if I did go with you." Eagle explained, "It is because I shot a deer yesterday and I need someone to bring it home while I go on from there to hunt." "You are asking a very pitiful person to do this," Skunk protested, and he worried about it all night.

In the morning Eagle told him, "Hurry now and get ready! We must get going. Do you think I should bring you food all the time without expecting you to do something in return? You won't have to go far, and you will be back very soon." So they set out together and they went far. "But you told me it was not far away," Skunk complained. "But we haven't come far," Eagle answered. "You certainly are no hunter." At last they arrived at Eagle's cache and there was the deer. Skunk packed up the meat and Eagle went on. However, Eagle took a roundabout path and started for home. He went along fast. Then he began to slash the ground with his wings. He slashed the ground everywhere, and everywhere he slashed he made a deep valley with high cliffs and deep gorges. Again, farther on, he slashed the ground and deep gorges appeared. Thus he went along gashing the surface of the land with his wings.

Skunk, meanwhile, had started for home. He came to the valleys and chasms. "The Eagle has discovered my wives, and, oh, just when the youngest one seemed to love me so much!" Skunk wept about his wives as he made his way slowly along. Eagle arrived ahead of Skunk at their lodge. He seized the Killdeer and bit them. Then he gathered up all his valuable possessions, including the Killdeer sisters, and moved out. He hauled his things to a cliff so inaccessible that nobody could ever reach him. Eagle feared Skunk and he knew that Skunk would search for him without fail, and if he found him would spray his scent on him. All the people recognized the Skunk's power as a doctor and no person cared to have any encounters with him. For this reason Eagle took possessions and all to a faraway hiding place.

At last, Skunk reached home and saw his things lying about. He noticed that all of Eagle's things and the Killdeer were missing and then he wept. "If I ever see Eagle I will squirt musk on him!" he vowed. Skunk was remorseful for a long time. He would go about, day after day, always looking for Eagle, but he was never able to find Eagle's tracks. He could not find them because Eagle had flown, not walked, away. Nevertheless, Skunk constantly watched for signs of Eagle during his wanderings.

One day during his travels, he saw a river nearby and went down to the bank to have a drink. He leaned forward to drink when suddenly he saw them all — Eagle and his five wives — there in the water. They were laughing. "So this is where he brought them! So they are living here in the water. No wonder I haven't been able to find them. Now I shall have my revenge,"

Skunk said to himself. Here he sprayed his scent into the water. That spot in the river suddenly went completely dry. Eagle and his wives disappeared also. Soon the water surged in again and Skunk looked. There they were in the same place, and were laughing, laughing at him it seemed.

Again he sprayed scent on them. That watery place became suddenly dry again and Eagle and his wives disappeared. But when the water flowed back in again he saw them all in the same place. He sprayed them with musk again and again, but each time the result was the same, they kept reappearing. Skunk completely exhausted himself and he started to ease the tension of his muscles by stretching. He threw back his head when suddenly he saw them above on the overhanging cliff. They were laughing and laughing at him. "Well, they were not in the water after all," he realized.

Now Skunk shouted up to Eagle, "Brother, throw down the eldest one for me." "Ha!" retorted Eagle. "That one is my most beloved." "Then the next oldest one," shouted Skunk. "That one is my most beloved." "Then the youngest one." "Well, then climb up here after her," replied Eagle. "Come after her yourself." The the youngest of the sisters began to weep. "You don't think much of me!" Eagle replied, "No, I am just lying to him."

Skunk shouted again, "How, brother, can I climb up there?" "Backwards," replied Eagle and Skunk began to back up the hill. Eagle quickly kindled a fire and put in a round stone to heat. Skunk climbed up slowly backwards, thinking all the while, "Just let me get near and I will squirt musk on them and kill every one." He was very near when Eagle suddenly picked up his hot stone, threw it, and hit Skunk with perfect accuracy. The stone tore through Skunk's body and came out through his mouth, carrying with it his musk sac. He suddenly found himself, without realizing how it had happened, on the rocks below. "Ugh!" he gasped, and right away he felt himself bereft of his power which was in his musk sac. He got up and searched all around for it, but it was nowhere to be found. Now he knew that it had floated away.

He built himself a raft from logs and quickly he got aboard and floated away with the current. "I am going to follow my musk sac no matter how far," he decided. He forgot all about Eagle and his wives. He floated along weeping and wailing, "My musk sac, my musk sac, my shamanistic power!" Down the river someone hailed him. "Yes, your musk sac came past here, but it was floating in the middle of the river and I was unable to salvage it for you." "I am grateful, nevertheless, and I will visit you when I come past again to show you my goodwill," Skunk shouted back.

He floated down the river on and on, constantly wailing, "My musk sac, my musk sac, my shamanistic power!" Again someone hailed him. It was a spirited woman, an Indian celery woman. She shouted, "As a matter of fact, your musk sac did float ashore here, but I told the people that it was your repulsive musk sac and they pushed it out into the current again." "My curse upon you! I will return past here seeking vengeance," Skunk shouted back. Many people at different places along the shore hailed Skunk as he floated past. Some of them had tried to recover the musk sac and to these Skunk shouted his gratitude and his promise to visit them later in a spirit of goodwill. Others had found his musk sac, but it revolted them and they set it afloat again. To these Skunk shouted his illwill and his threat to return in a spirit of vengeance.

Finally Skunk had drifted to the far lower reaches of the river. There he went ashore and started travelling by land. He was going along the road when he happened to step on and break Meadowlark's leg. She cried out in distress and Skunk said to her, "Aunt, tell me where my musk sac is and I will make you a leg of brushwood." She replied, "Very well. They are holding your musk sac in a place where it will be very difficult for you to recover it. The people there have an orphan baby and they are using your musk sac to amuse and pacify it. They are rolling your musk sac back and forth and it goes sparkle, sparkle, and the infant baby is pacified thereby. They are rolling it back and forth and I do not think that you can recover your musk sac." "Yes, Aunt," Skunk said, "you have informed me well." Then he made a wooden leg for Meadowlark and went on. He stopped along the way and made himself a makeshift musk sac from a pungent shrub. This new musk sac was very weak but it was better than none at all. He continued on down the river.

One night, as he went along, he saw some people ahead. "Oh, there are many people." Suddenly he saw something shooting back and forth with a sparkle that was just like flashes of lightning. "Oh, it's mine, my special power!" Skunk exclaimed. Then he thought, "How am I going to recover it? Just how am I going to exchange with them? When they cast the musk sac in this direction I am going to take it and roll back in its place the musk sac which I made of the shrub." The musk sac rolled along sparkling. Skunk crouched low in the right position and the musk sac shot across the ground and ran straight into Skunk's body.

At the same moment Skunk hurled the shrub musk sac back to the people, and away he scampered. "If they find me they will kill me," he told himself and so he hurried up the valley. But the people continued to send the musk sac, the shrub one, back and forth and it did sparkle a few times, but it began slowly to dim and finally it went out. The people tried it again but the same thing happened. "What has happened to it?" they exclaimed. "Somebody has done something to it." They kept casting it back and forth, but there was no sparkle. Then one person happened to remember, "I thought I saw Skunk around here awhile ago. Probably he has taken the musk sac from us."

By this time, Skunk was hiking along far up the valley already. "Now I shall revenge myself on all those who found my musk sac so repulsive." He came to a longhouse and said to the people, "I am just on my way from the powerful shamans down the river, but I will stop a little while and sing you some shaman songs." The people gathered and Skunk sprayed them with musk. He made them all foul and pungent to the taste. These were the plant people like Indian celery and ginseng, who sent his musk sac farther down the river.

Skunk went on up the valley. There he arrived at another lodge where many people were dancing a spirit dance. Skunk thought, "I will have revenge here also." He addressed the people, "I am just on my way from the powerful shamans down the river, but I will stop a little while to sing some shaman songs for you." The people gathered to listen, but there happened to be a Raven present, and when Skunk began to sing, the Raven sensed Skunk's treachery and he sang out a warning, "Oh, oh, Skunk is going to spray us with musk!" This completely bewildered Skunk and at the same time it constricted his musk sac so he could not spray his scent. Skunk protested, "Disrespectful youth! I've never done such a thing to anyone." But there he sat squirming on his haunches unable to squirt musk on the people. At last he became exhausted trying to discharge his musk and got up and left.

He went on up the valley and came to another longhouse. He recognized these people as those who had tried to recover his musk sac for him, so he went inside and found all the people dancing. "I am just on my way from the powerful shamans," he told them. Then he danced and sang for the people and they all watched, enraptured. Then Skunk left them and continued up the valley.

He was going along when a Bobolink saw him. "Oh, I am about to meet a powerful shaman. I believe I had better play dead," the Bobolink said to himself. When Skunk came upon the Bobolink lying there, he said, "Oh, brother, I see that they have killed you. The shamans in their envy have attacked and killed you. You were always such a proud fellow and you were always well-dressed. You were so very, very proud and that is why the shamans were always envious, that is why they killed you," Skunk chattered as he picked up the Bobolink and tossed it into his basket which he carried on his back.

Skunk was going along his way when he saw a Wolf rapidly approaching. In alarm, Skunk lay back on his basket to hide the Bobolink he carried. He did not want the Wolf to see the dead Bobolink in his basket. The Wolf approached and Skunk said to him, "Hello, brother, so you are going down the valley. I would advise you not to come up to me, but pass around me at a safe distance because I am on my way from a meeting of the powerful shamans and I might cast a bad influence over you if you come too close." "Yes, brother," replied the Wolf, "I will do as you say since you are travelling along from a meeting of the powerful ones." In the same way Skunk met the third and then the fourth of the Wolf brothers and they, too, passed by casually.

But soon Skunk saw the youngest Wolf approaching at a fast pace and he fell back on his basket as he had done before. This time Skunk was gripped by fear as he addressed the approaching Wolf in these words, "Hello, brother, I am just going along, but I am on my way from a meeting of the powerful shamans. Do not come near me because I might cast a bad influence over you." All this time Skunk was saying to himself, "Oh, he is sure to find the Bobolink in my basket. I wish he would be respectful and pass me as his brothers did." However, the Wolf came straight toward him and said, "Yes, but I haven't seen you for such a long time! Give me your hand, let us shake hands!"

And he rushed right up despite Skunk's protesting words, "No, brother! Stop, brother! I am on my way from the powerful ones!" "Yes, but give me your hand!" the Wolf insisted as he seized Skunk by the hand and, at the same time, looked into the basket at the supposedly dead Bobolink. Now the Wolf said, "So be it, you are just travelling along," and with that he went on down the valley. Skunk mumbled wretchedly, "I knew that the youngest one would not respect me. Now he has seen me carrying this dead Bobolink."

Skunk continued his way up the valley. After a time he began to talk to himself about feeling brave, forgetting at the same time how frightened he had been a few moments before. He began to sing, "There is nothing I fear, there is just nothing I fear! If a boulder should roll down at me as I pass by I would simply squirt musk on it and blast it into countless pieces. And if at the same time a big pine tree should fall on me, I would simply squirt musk on it and blast it into countless pieces. There is nothing I fear, there is just one thing I fear!"

He was suddenly gripped by fear at the thought of the thing he feared, so he scampered up the valley making his usual sound as he ran. Soon he composed himself, though, and he began again. "I only fear one thing, only one thing!" But again fright overwhelmed him and up the valley he ran pell-mell. Then he thought, "Oh, why did I have to think of it! There is only one thing I fear and now I am going to say it. Now I am going to say it!" But he only became frightened again. "Oh, why did I have to even think of it! But now I am ready to say it," he said. Meanwhile, the Bobolink in his basket who had been pretending to be dead all this time, was listening to all of Skunk's prattle. "Oh, I wish he would name it! Oh, I wish he would name that thing which he fears!" the Bobolink said to himself.

Finally Skunk said, "Now, whatever prompted me to think of it in the first place, there is just one thing I fear and that is . . . whistling!" And with that utterance he dashed up the valley terror-stricken. Bobolink knew now what Skunk feared and he began to whistle from the basket, but whistled so that it seemed to come from afar. "Ugh!" gasped Skunk almost prostrated, and he began to run. He fled up the valley until he became so tired he could go no further so he said to himself, "I am tired. Let me hang my brother up here while I go on and later I will return for him." So Skunk stripped off all of the Boblink's adornments and hung him on a thorn bush. As Skunk went on, the Bobolink whistled at him and away Skunk scampered panic stricken. The Bobolink whistled at him with a final strong blast and Skunk disappeared up the valley.

In time, Skunk forgot his fear. He finally came to a shady place and thought, "Ah, here is a good shady place. Now let me stop and play the stick-game." He gathered some chunks of rotten wood which he put up in a large circle. Then he took five more chunks of wood to represent his wives and he seated himself amongst them. He turned to his youngest wife and said, "Move over a little. You always crowd me! You are hampering my play. Move over!" Then Skunk arranged the rotten chunks of wood in two rows, each chunk facing an opponent of the other side. Now he piled all the ornaments, the shell and bead adornments which he had taken from the Bobolink, between the opposing sides. When everything was properly arranged, Skunk began to sing, "Play the stick-game with yourself White Skunk! Play the stick-game with yourself!" Now and then during his song Skunk would scold one of his wives, "Move over a little, you! You will cause me to lose, and nobody can win from me because I am travelling along from a meeting of the powerful ones." Skunk wriggled about on his haunches talking and singing to his chunks of wood, and he gave himself up completely to the wild enchantment and thrill of the game.

125

Meanwhile, the Wolves came back up the valley looking for him. The youngest Wolf had overtaken his brothers and told them, "Skunk was carrying along a poor Bobolink," so they came looking for Skunk. They heard his stick-game song, crept up stealthily and saw Skunk there squirming about on his haunches playing the stick-game by himself. The youngest Wolf crept up behind Skunk, and deftly planted his foot on Skunk's tail and, at the same time, seized him by the nape of the neck. Skunk did not stir, he did not move a muscle.

The youngest Wolf then said to his brother, "Fetch me a wooden club and let me club him to death." This aroused Skunk and he protested, "What am I, an old woman that you would club me to death like this? Step aside and let us meet with bare hands!" "Yes, as if your brave talk were not in terms of your musk sac!" the young Wolf retorted, and turning to his brothers insisted, "Hurry, give me a club!" They handed him a club and he clubbed poor Skunk to death. Then the Wolves took all the beads, ornaments, and valuable possessions which Skunk himself had stolen.

This is the end of this story about White Skunk.

How Bear Led a Boy Astray

A boy was out hunting when Bear captured him. She took him into her den and kept him there for a long, long time. One day she said to him, "You are going home to your mother and father. You are to go home for only a short time and then you will return again. Bear prepared a lunch for him. She prepared camas roots for his lunch because it was the root digging season and she repeated her instructions, "You are just going to visit them briefly. Then tomorrow or the day after you will return. Now, you must sing when you are about to arrive."

The young man's father and mother had come to believe that their son was dead. Bear gave him a song and he set out. He travelled along and when he was about to arrive he began to sing, "The widow has led me astray. The widow has led me astray." His parents heard the song and they rejoiced to find that their son was alive and that he had returned home, but the young man stayed with his father and mother for just a few days. Then he said to them, "I came only to visit you and now I am going back." It happened that the people there were catching many salmon and they gave the young man a large supply of salmon to take with him.

He set out for home and arrived at the bear den to find that Bear was digging roots. The young man decided to prepare food for Bear, so he broiled a salmon for her. Bear soon arrived and said, "Oh, salmon! That is wonderful!" "There is some I have already broiled for you," the young man told her. "Oh, it is overdone! I can't eat it like that," she told him. "Then I will eat it myself and you can cook some in whatever way you like."

Then Bear took a salmon and sprinkled it with dust to season it. "This is how it should be done. Oh, this is such good salmon," she said. Then the young man said to her, "The people told me that we should come to their place because they are catching many salmon." "But there are so many people there. It would be embarrassing," Bear said. "They have invited us. We could go just for a short time," the young man replied. "Very well then, we will go," she consented. They prepared for their visit. Bear went out to dig camas roots to take with them and they were ready to go at last.

When they arrived, there were many, many people encamped and they were making merry. There were all kinds of social activities and Bear's husband joined right in the festivity. He danced and he participated in all their various activities. One day Bear said to her husband, "Let us go home now." "Not just yet, let us go later," the young man replied. Bear persisted, but her husband seemed most reluctant to leave and he kept putting her off.

At last Bear became angry. She knew that certain maidens were making merry with her husband, so she decided to kill them. She went out of camp into the brush. It was the season in which chokecherries and serviceberries were ripening, and the maidens used to go out frequently to pick and eat berries. Bear saw a party of maidens walking away from camp. She circled around them and lay down ahead of them in the bushes near their path. She could hear them very clearly talking excitedly to one another. "Bear's husband was giving me such special attention at the dance," one maiden was saying.

When Bear heard her husband's name mentioned a sudden deep hatred possessed her. "This is why he is always so unwilling to go! This is why he is always telling me, 'We will go later, we will go later.' " Bear mumbled in deep anger. The maidens came, and when they were near her, Bear jumped up and rushed at them. She bit one to death. She rushed at another one and bit her to death, and she killed all five of the maidens. Then she dug a pit and buried them.

She was covered with blood and even though she washed herself thoroughly, there was a pungent odor of blood about her. Finally, she tied a bandage around her head and went home and lay down as if she were ill. Her husband came into their lodge soon and observing her apparent condition asked, "What is the matter?" There was a heavy odor of blood in the lodge. "My head aches and I was bleeding from the nose. I feel as if I am about to become very ill. I believe that we should go home," Bear replied.

In the meanwhile, the people about camp had noticed the absence of the maidens and at once they suspected Bear. They searched for the maidens and at once found where Bear had buried them. "There is no question about it now, Bear has killed them," the people agreed. Coyote pronounced judgment. "Bear has killed those five sisters. This woman, who is a newcomer, may not do such a thing and she, too, must be killed," he ruled. The people went to Bear's husband and said to him, "The salmon are not running. We have not caught a single one lately. But we believe that your wife is a powerful shaman, and if she took a sweatbath the salmon might run again."

The husband told Bear what had been proposed. "This is embarrassing," she exclaimed. "Yes, but they are placing all their faith in you and they have confidence in nobody else. If you should cause a run of salmon, we will receive a large quantity of dried salmon to take home." "But it would be so embarrassing!" repeated Bear. "Then go into the sweathouse fully clothed," offered her husband. "All right, then, I will do this for them," Bear consented at last.

128

The people heated stones and Bear went to the sweathouse fully clothed. The red-hot stones had already been piled inside and the people made a hole in the roof of the sweat lodge directly above the hot stones. Everybody gathered around. Then they began to pour water through the hole and the red-hot stones gave off a terrific heat. Bear said to herself, "They are going to kill me!" She began to writhe and struggle, but the people poured more water through the hole and then they crowded around and sat on the sweathouse to hold Bear inside. She struggled fiercely, but the suffocating heat was too much and she was suffocated. Then the people dragged her out of the sweathouse. The people continued to live there.

Wild Goat Carries a Woman Away

A man and his wife lived by themselves, and the man left his wife alone for a time. She would go out to dig roots every day and she would make root-loaf from the roots. One day she returned home from her root digging to discover that all of her root-loaf was gone. "I wonder who could have taken my root-loaf," she said to herself in amazement. She glanced about the lodge and discovered a large quantity of salmon in the back part of the room. She wondered, "Who can have taken my root-loaf and left all this dried salmon for me?" She ate very heartily of the salmon and was glad to have received it, because salmon was difficult to get.

The next day she went out, dug more roots, and made another supply of root-loaf. A few days passed and then again, upon returning from her root digging, she found that her root-loaf had been taken and that a pile of dried salmon had been left. "Who is doing this? I believe I will hide and wait for them next time and see who comes," she decided. She counted the days that seemed to be the interval between visits, and now she thought, "Today they will probably come again."

She stayed in her lodge this time instead of going out to dig roots and waited. Presently she heard them coming. They were shouting to one another as they came. "Oh, they are children," the woman realized and she kept very still in her hiding place. "My brother's wife always leaves mine over there," another said. Now all the children, and there were many of them, came into the lodge. The woman was still hidden as the children rummaged around in the back part of the lodge saying, "My brother's wife just always leaves my portion here." Then one happened to uncover the woman and he began to squeal in sudden terror.

The other children looked and became terrified and began to squeal and rush for the door. They crowded one another out through the door and away they ran. The woman called to them, "Come back, I'm not going to hurt you! Wait, let me talk to you! Stop! Why do you run away?" But the children ran on. They had left all their salmon in the lodge and ran away empty handed. Several days passed and the woman continued to dig roots and make root-loaf. She exhausted her supply of dried salmon and the children did not come again. "I scared them very badly and they will not come again," she said to herself.

She continued to live there and one day she went out to dig as usual. After she had dug for awhile she sat down to rest. She looked away and saw a thundercloud looming on the horizon. It was so beautiful there extending across the sky that she felt a deep loneliness. "Ah, I wish that the cloud would come to me! It is so beautiful!" she murmured. Presently she forgot about the cloud and began to dig roots again. "I will dig for a little while longer and then I will go home."

Soon she said to herself, "That is enough," and she went to get her pile of roots, but there sitting on her roots was a great horned-buck, a wild goat. The woman said to him, "Go away! You are sitting on my roots. Go away and let me pack them." The goat did not move. Then he said to her, "I am that for which you were longing. You called me and I have come." The woman said, "My husband's brother, go away." "Not my husband's brother! Make our kinship different," the ram retorted. Then the woman in desperation began to call him by various kinship terms but he would not move. He kept

130

replying, "Refer to me differently." If she said, "My elder sister's son, get up," he would answer, "Not my elder sister's son!"

The woman knew that he wanted to be called husband. At last she decided, "I will say that, then, but I certainly will not go with him." So she said to the wild goat, "My husband, get up," and he jumped to his feet. The woman gathered up and packed her roots thinking all the while, "I shall certainly not go with him." The goat stood nearby watching her. Presently she finished her packing and stood up and a second later she found herself sitting between the goat's horns. There she sat powerless, pack and all, between the goat's horns and he started off, carrying her away as his captured wife. They travelled along and the woman thought to herself, "Oh, how it used to be that I could drink at a good, clear, pebbled place in the stream!" Then the goat said to her, "Part my hair there beside you." She parted his hair and beheld a beautiful stream flowing over a pebbled beach.

They travelled on and on to unknown parts and finally arrived. Then he set her down and said, "Your sisters-in-law will come to get you. Stay right here." The ram went to his lodge and told his sisters, "Go fetch your sister-in-law." One of the sisters came out and found the woman. "Come along, let us go home," she told her. They went to the wild goat's lodge and that became the woman's new home.

One day the sisters said to their sister-in-law, "We always go out to gather grass and that will be your task also." These sisters used to go across the river by canoe and cut grass to take home. Now the woman took up her assigned work and she would go across the river every day to gather grass. Her husband, the wild goat, did nothing but sweatbathe. He was continually sweatbathing. However, he had told his sisters, "You must always keep careful watch on your sister-in-law."

Now it happened that the man who had been this woman's first husband learned that his wife had been carried away by the wild ram. He decided "I will go and take her away from that wild goat." He set out and as he went along, he happened to step on and break Meadowlark's leg. "How do you expect to find your wife!" the Meadowlark scolded the man. But he said to her, "Aunt, tell me where she is and later I will make a new leg of brushwood for you." "Well, your wife is in a very difficult situation. She is in a very bad place, and is being held against her will. Although she does go across a river every day to cut grass, her sisters-in-law always watch her very closely because they are very, very suspicious of her." "You have informed me well," the man said and made a new leg for her. He went on and arrived at last during the night at a place that seemed to him to be the place described by Meadowlark.

He hid in the deep grass. He stayed there until dawn and at last he saw her push out into the river in a canoe. He watched her paddle across, come ashore, and begin to cut grass very close to where he lay hidden. In a little while he spoke up, "Ouch, wild goat mistress, you are pulling my hair!" Oh, how she jumped in sudden fright. Then the man, realizing that the wild goat sisters must be watching, said to her, "Look at your hand quickly," so the woman looked at her hand. The man explained, "The sisters will think, 'She jumps because she cut her hand.' " The woman continued to look at her hand while the man talked to her, "And then you will take me home with you." She replied, "There is no possible way, it is difficult." "If you place me in a bunch of grass which you will take for yourself, you will succeed. When you get home tell the others, 'I have brought this bundle of grass for myself because our bed is very hard and I need this much for myself.' " The woman replied, "I am very much afraid of them, but if you believe this is the thing to do then I will take you."

Meanwhile, across the river the goat sisters were having an argument. One was saying, "I'm sure that she was startled by a person." The others replied, "No, she only cut herself. She is looking at her hand." Their argument continued on through the day and they decided finally to settle it by questioning the woman. When evening came, the woman loaded the grass into her canoe and started home. She put the man in a separate bundle of grass which she placed beside her.

She paddled slowly because her hand was heavily bandaged. As she paddled across the river, the man gave her final instructions. "Tonight you must be very affectionate toward the ram and he will fall asleep quickly." The woman reached the shore and her sisters-in-law rushed down to meet her. "You were frightened and jumped because of a person?" they asked. "No, I cut my hand very painfully," the woman told them. "There, that is what I told you!" one exclaimed. The woman added, "I am taking this bunch of grass for myself. Our bed is very hard." The sisters replied indifferently, "Take it, then."

The wild goat and his wife lived in a semi-pit lodge and the sisters had a separate lodge for themselves. The woman carried her former husband home in the bundle of grass and set the bundle aside, but certainly not to use for bedding. Now she and the wild ram spent the evening and she caressed him with more affection than usual. He became drowsy soon and dropped off to sleep and began to snore.

Then the woman unwrapped her husband who took a knife and cut the wild goat's throat. Then he turned to the woman and said, "Get ready quickly for we are leaving." She got ready while the man cut off the ram's head and set the body in such a position that the buttocks were uppermost and pointing out from the door. Then they went. The man carried the ram's head, got into a canoe, and paddled out into the river. When they reached the middle they threw the head overboard. Then they paddled across to the opposite shore and there the man gave the canoe a shove with his foot and sent it back across the river. Then they set out and travelled all night.

At the wild goat's camp, the sisters got up at dawn and prepared breakfast. They began to wonder about the ram when he did not appear. "How is this that they are still asleep? They are always up and doing things by this time. One of you go to awaken them," one of the sisters said. One of them went off to ram's semi-pit lodge and there, as she approached, she was suddenly stricken with terror because she saw the ram lying in the doorway with his buttocks pointing out.

She ran back and shouted to her sisters, "He is dead! I told you it was a person that frightened the woman yesterday!" All the sisters went to see and found that the ram was indeed dead. Then they began to search for his head. They looked and looked and at last one saw a faint blur deep in the water. "There is his head in the water," she said. They began to dive after it but the water was so deep they couldn't quite reach it. They continued to dive but every time they would begin to suffocate and strangle. At last, after many, many attempts one of the sisters managed to reach the head and pull it up.

Meanwhile, the man and his wife went on and travelled far. In time, the woman gave birth to a baby, a young wild goat. The man said to her, "Throw it away!" but the woman refused. "No, I love it." The man insisted, "Hurry, throw it away!" "No, I love it," she repeated. So the man went off and left her. She thought, "Anyway, I will not return to the wild goat." She made a cradleboard and bound her baby on it. The baby had hair all over its body. It resembled its father in body, but its face was that of a person. The mother kept it on the cradleboard and bound her baby on it and every little while she would unbind it. The hair began to peel off, first from around the neck and then from the body, and finally all the hair peeled off and the baby was white.

Still the woman travelled on and on, camping every night. One day she stepped on Meadowlark's leg and broke it. "Where do you expect to find your husband!" Meadowlark berated her. The woman said, "Aunt, inform me and then I will make a leg of brushwood for you." Meadowlark replied, "You are travelling along a very difficult road. It is a dangerous way and who can tell whether you will get through or not. You have three ordeals to pass through. First you will arrive at a big crevice that will open and close continually, and out of that crevice will be leaping big tongues of flame. If you run across at the right moment, just when the crevice closes, you will get through all right, but if you should fall in, that will be your death. You will go from there to a place beyond and you will meet two boys. Just as you approach you must sing and the boys, hearing you, will rush out to meet you and bite you. They will bite and watch your face and if you make the slightest grimace, that will be your death. When you have passed these boys you go to the third ordeal, the skull brothers. There are five of them and they, too, are killers. If you succeed in passing them, however, your life will be saved, you will belong to the land of the living. As I said before, yours is a very dangerous road." The woman then made a brushwood leg for

Meadowlark and said to her, "Yes, aunt, you have informed me well."

The woman travelled on and soon she arrived at the place where the fiery fissure was opening and closing. Fire blazed from the gaping crevice, but she remembered Meadowlark's advice. She watched carefully and just as the crevice closed, she ran across. "I have passed the first," she mumbled. She went on.

Presently she heard a wailing. "It must be the children," she thought. She approached closer. "Let them bite if they like," she said to her herself. Then she began to sing, "My beloved children got lost here. Two brothers got lost." She continued singing and the boys ran to meet her. They said to each other, "Probably it is our mother." They rushed up to the woman and began to bite her. They watched her eyes for a grimace by which they would know, "She is not our mother." However, the woman showed no expression of pain, but gazed about nonchalantly. "It is certain, then, then she is our mother," the boys told each other.

They stopped biting and asked the woman, "Mother, is that your baby?" "Yes, it is my baby," she told them. "But he is so very white. How did our brother get so white?" the boys asked. "Oh, I just did something to him that you boys could not do," she replied. "What did you do to him?" they wanted to know. "Well," said the woman, "I only dug a hole, a pit, and I started a fire in it and heated some stones. Then I smeared the baby with pitch and threw him into the fire in the pit. I rolled him about with a forked stick and immediately his skin began to peel off and he turned white." "Mother, do that to us, too," the boys exclaimed. "Well, if you insist. But you must gather some wood," she told them.

So the boys ran off to gather wood and the woman dug a hole. She dug it very deep and wide as such a pit should be. Then she started a fire and heated stones until they became red hot. The boys smeared themselves with pitch. When everything was ready the woman said to them, "The fire pit is just right now and you boys must jump in together because if one should go ahead of the other your coloring would be

135

different, that is, one will be white and the other dirty and smeary." The boys hesitated. They looked at the red hot stones and they became frightened and undecided. The woman thought, "I do hope they won't be afraid." She told them again, "Now just jump into the fire together." The boys flung themselves into the pit and how their pitch-smeared bodies blazed! The woman held them down by the necks with her forked stick and in a few moments they burned to ashes. "Why did you think, 'We can be murderers'? The human race comes in a short time and then it will be said, 'Here is where a leader went astray.' "

Then the woman went on. "I have only one more ordeal to pass through," she thought. She travelled far and finally came upon a sweathouse. "Oh, here is a sweathouse," she said to herself. "Let me spend the night here. It is so good and warm inside." She entered the sweathouse, put her baby to sleep, and prepared to stay overnight. After a while she heard a noise, she heard something going click-clack, click-clack, click-clack, click-clack. Then she heard it closer and suddenly in through the door came bouncing the five skull brothers. They began to chase one another about the room and as they ran they bounced about, click-clack, click-clack, click-clack. In all the commotion, they happened to run over the woman's baby and crushed it to death. Nevertheless, the woman remained with the skull brothers and became their wife.

In the course of time, she had another baby, a young skull. One day the skulls informed her, "There are many people camping across the river," and they decided to go across and visit. They summoned a canoe from the other side to ferry them across. The canoe arrived and the woman got aboard, but the skulls, instead of getting into the canoe, plunged into the water, plop, and disappeared. Even the young skull plunged into the river. The woman alone was paddled across. She landed and went ashore, but the skulls, too, appeared and they went to the people's camp.

There the people were making merry while nearby their children were enjoying themselves at play. The young skull went over to join the children in their games. He began to bounce around among them when suddenly, smack, he bumped one. The child began to cry, but the young skull was having a glorious time. Presently he bumped other children and soon he had them all crying, the young coyotes and all. He would bounce around and suddenly, smack, he would bump someone on the head. At last Coyote became provoked. "What manner of person is this you have brought among us!" he raved to the people. Every little while he would find one of his children crying and he became very angry.

Then at mealtime, as soon as the food was served, the skulls would plunge right into the dish and consume every bit. Coyote plotted against them and told various persons, "There will be a council-smoke in my lodge." The people assembled and Coyote addressed them. "These skulls have been tormenting us unmercifully, so we must take action against them. Let us use that cliff. We will say, 'Tear apart and crumble that cliff for us.'" The people agreed, "That is what we will have them do." The woman, too, was favorably disposed to this plan, even though she was the skulls' wife. "Do whatever you wish. I will not hate you for it," she told them.

So one morning Coyote went to the skulls and said to them, "You are very powerful and we, the people, have wanted for a long time to have that cliff crumbled to pieces. We believe that you, being so powerful, can do it. You will do this only out of pity for us." The skulls replied, "Well, we can try. We don't know but it looks like a very difficult thing to do." Then the skulls came forth to crush the cliff. The eldest brother tried first. He rushed furiously at the cliff, hurled himself against the rock and he cracked open. He was killed.

The second brother tried next. He rushed fiercely, hurtled, and was cracked open and killed. Then the third, fourth, and fifth of the brothers tried desperately, only to be destroyed. Even the young skull hurled himself at the cliff and was killed. In this manner, all the skulls were exterminated by destroying themselves. Then the woman dwelt there.

Coyote and His Guests

Coyote and his wife Mouse had a child, a boy. One day Coyote said to his son, "Boy-child, let us visit your uncle Elk." They arrived at Elk's lodge. "Brother, we just thought we would come to see you," Coyote explained. They began to talk about various things and they told each other stories. Elk's wife was there at work sewing. They had a son, too. Presently Elk went over to his wife and with a knife cut a piece of dress off her back. He broiled it and it smelled delicious. Elk said to Coyote, "I just haven't a thing in the way of food, friend, only this, but eat it." "What is this? I should eat old worn clothing!" Coyote thought. Then young Coyote began to eat, too, and he ate very much. Soon there was only a little bit of food left and Coyote decided, "I will just taste it then. Oh, it is very, very good." So he ate all that was left. Then he scolded his son, "You are showing the habits of eating you develop at home! My brother and I are still telling each other stories and you eat up all the food!" After a while Coyote said to Elk, "Yes, brother, it has been very good to tell each other stories and sometime you must visit me at my lodge."

Days passed by and then Elk said to his son, "Coyote told us to come and see him sometime. Let us go now." They arrived at Coyote's rye grass lodge and Mouse said to herself, "Why does Coyote have them come? He will, without fail, do something stupid again." Elk and his son had arrived and Coyote said, "Brother, I am very glad that you have come. This is just the way I live." Coyote talked on and then they told each other stories again. After a while Coyote stood up and went over to his wife who was occupied there at something or other. He took his knife and ripped off a piece of her dress and boiled it. The piece of her dress shriveled at once. Mouse said to herself, "Imitator." "Mine never did anything like this before," Coyote exclaimed for Elk's benefit. But now Elk took pity on Coyote and he cut a piece out of his own back and put it on to broil. Then he said to his son, "Let us go now. We have caused

Coyote to do things very poorly. They returned home while Coyote and his family ate well.

Days passed and Coyote said to his son, "Let us go to visit your uncle Fish-Hawk." They arrived at Fish-Hawk's lodge and Coyote said, "Brother, we have come to visit you. How are you getting along from day to day?" They sat down and talked about many things for a long time. After a while Fish-Hawk got up and went outside. He cut a wild cherry bush of about the thickness of a digging stick and he took it into the lodge. He bent the stick into a circular form and tied the ends together, then imbedded it in the coals.

Coyote and Fish-Hawk talked on and at last Fish-Hawk said, "We haven't anything to eat but this." He uncovered the stick he had put in the coals and took out a ring of sausage perfectly cooked and sizzling. Then he went outside where the boys were playing, for Fish-Hawk, too, had a son. He climbed up a big fir tree that stood near the lodge, perched there on one of the limbs for a few moments, gave his call, then swooped straight down through a hole in the ice. He emerged in a few moments holding a salmon.

Then he proceeded to broil the salmon. "There isn't a thing to eat, but here you are," he told Coyote. But Coyote turned to his son and said, "You eat! Am I supposed to eat wild cherry wood and winter salmon?" The young Coyote ate heartily and Coyote talked on. When the young Coyote had consumed almost all of the food Coyote thought, "Let me just taste it." He cut off a little piece of the fat and tasted it. Oh, how good it was. Then he gulped down the rest of it and then scolded his son. "You are showing the habits of eating you develop at home! My brother and I are still talking and you eat all the food." Presently Coyote said to Fish-Hawk, "Brother, you must come to see me at my lodge sometime." The guests returned home.

Then days passed. At last Fish-Hawk said to his son, "Coyote asked us to visit him, so let us go." They went to call on Coyote. "Yes, brother, so you have come. This is how we live." Coyote greeted Fish-Hawk. They began to talk and presently Coyote got up and went outside. He cut down a wild cherry bush and brought it into the lodge. He bent it around, tied the ends, and put it into the coals to cook. Coyote's wife, Mouse, said to herself, "The imitator, whom did he see doing that? He is the doer of all foolhardy things."

Coyote and his guests talked about various things when suddenly that piece of wild cherry wood hurled itself from the fire because the string that bound the two ends together had burned through. Ashes, coals, and fire were flung in every direction and the stick hurled itself across the room and struck Mouse squarely on the back. "Oh!" she yelled in sudden fright. Coyote exclaimed, "What could have happened: It is very strange, nothing like this ever occurred before." Fish-Hawk then took pity on Coyote, went out and brought back a wild cherry stick which he bent, tied, and put into the coals.

Then Coyote went outside. A big fir tree stood near the river and there was a hole in the ice directly below the branches. Coyote climbed up into the tree and young Coyote shouted to his mother, "Oh, come and see! Father is climbing up the tree! "Hush! As if it were the first time you have seen me do this. You always say the most foolish things," Coyote shouted from above. Then he climbed up and perched on a limb, gave the cry of a fish-hawk and suddenly hurled himself down. He dived for the hole in the ice, but he missed and instead landed on the edge of the hole with a thud. He had almost killed himself.

Then Fish-Hawk took pity on him again and he jumped up into the tree, perched there for a moment, gave a few calls, and he dived. He plunged straight through the hole in the ice and reappeared holding a salmon. He handed it to Coyote and, turning to his son, said, "Let us go home now. We have already made Coyote look bad."

So they returned home. Coyote had plenty of good food now, but both Coyote and his wife, Mouse, were confined to bed, one suffering from the effects of the fall and the other bruised from having been struck by the hot wild cherry stick.

Coyote and Elbow-Child

Fox and Coyote each had five daughters who lived in the maidens' pitlodge. It was wintertime. Fox and Coyote lived in a conical lodge. It came about that Coyote developed a lump on his elbow. He said to his daughters, "Daughters, daughters, there is a lump on my elbow and it hurts me. Open it for me." They pricked it open and a child, a boy, emerged. He was a very lovable baby boy and the daughters loved him and fondled him. One day the boy suddenly died because the daughters had fondled him too much. The boy was a coyote and he would laugh with a cackle, and he died from overlaughing.

Coyote grieved very deeply, and he wept. "Elbow-Child was going to be a chief. He was going to have an engaging personality. He was going to be a prodigious performer!" Coyote wailed. He sang his lamentation and he wept. Then he became angry at all the others. In his hatred for the girls he poured water into their lodge, and since it was cold, ice formed from the water. The door froze solid and could not be opened, even though Fox tugged at it with all his might. Then Fox dug a little hole through the roof of the lodge and he was able to pass food through to the maidens. But Coyote, unmindful of everything else, did nothing but wander around singing about his Elbow-Child. The maidens became hungry and then, one by one, they began to die of starvation because the door remained frozen shut.

One day Coyote's eldest daughter shouted to Fox through the hole in the roof, "What time of year has it become, Uncle?" Fox replied, "The sunflowers are just beginning to bloom." Fox continued to push little bits of food through the hole. The eldest daughter called to him again and told him, "Now I am here alone. All the others have died." Fox was grief-stricken and he wept and wept. Coyote said to him, "What are you weeping about? You weren't weeping when Elbow-Child died! In him we had a young chieftain."

One day the maiden said to Fox, "Uncle, I am telling you this. If I ever get out of here I am going to leave you because I feel very bad. I am heartsick over the death of my sisters. Yes, I will leave you." Finally, after many days, the door began to yield to Fox's constant tugging, and Coyote's surviving daughter got out. She said to Fox, "I am leaving you now, Uncle. I am angry at my father and I must go. I shall travel toward the setting sun, but later I will be going past here. That will be the beginning of summer. You will hear me coming, for I will come with fire and I will sing as I come. But do not fear me. I will be going past here just to see you, to visit you in a spirit of goodwill." The maiden held her sisters' hair which she had cut off. "I am taking this hair, Uncle, and now I am leaving you." Then she went. Fox pined deeply, but Coyote still wept about his Elbow-Child.

Fox began to await the arrival of the maiden and one day he heard her coming. She came in a mass of fire. "That is what she told me, 'I will come with fire.'" She came like a huge rolling ball of fire and came singing, "Fire will leap over the pitiful old man. Fire will take the hateful old man!" They heard her coming and singing, and Coyote became frightened. "Here comes my child. She speaks of me as the pitiful old man and of you as the hateful one," he told Fox. But Fox said nothing. When she got quite close, Coyote said in alarm, "Let us run! You will be burned!" "No," Fox replied, "even if I burn I am staying here." He remembered the maiden's parting words, "You must not be frightened when I arrive with fire." Coyote fled.

The fire came upon Fox and the maiden spoke to him. "I am on my way toward the sunrise, but now I am going to chase my father. I will burn him because he has caused me great suffering. The death of my sisters has caused me deep suffering. For that I will have his life. Now I am leaving you and you will never see me again." The mass of fire went on in the direction Coyote had fled. Coyote had run away in a tremendous burst of speed. He had said to himself, "Run with the intensity of a tendon broken from tautness!" And he ran quickly. Nevertheless, the maiden overtook him and she burned him to death and then the fire rolled on.

142

Fox spent a few days in deep loneliness. He pined because his comrade Coyote was gone. One day he decided, "I am going to search for my comrade." He went out to look for his friend and as he wandered about he began to say to himself, "I wonder where my comrade's chin is bleaching in the sun?" He went along repeating this to himself. Suddenly he heard, "I-wonder-where-my-comrade's-chin-is-bleaching-in-the- sun?" He heard it as a fast whisper. "Where did that come from?" Fox exclaimed to himself. He listened.

Then he said again, "I wonder where my comrade's chin is bleaching in the sun?" He heard immediately, "I-wonder-where-my-comrade's-chin-is-bleaching-in-the-sun?" Fox looked all around when he happened to see a slight puff of dust. "He seems to be here," he thought. Then he said it again, "I wonder where my comrade's chin is bleaching in the sun?" He located the spot and scraped away the ashes. "Here are his bones, all right," he observed. Then he gathered up all of Coyote's bones and after arranging them properly, straddled them five times and Coyote stood up. Then they went home and lived there again, umindful of all that had happened.

Shoshone Myths

Iron-Man

Iron-Man, the father of the white people, lived on the water. Wolf, the father of the Indians, lived underground. Wolf asked his son to visit his friend Iron-Man. The young man traveled across the water until he reached Iron-Man's house. Iron-Man shook hands with the youth and invited his father to visit him. "We shall see which one of us can beat the other in making guns." Wolf's son told his father of Iron-Man's invitation and Wolf got ready to go. Iron-Man locked up his house and sat down inside.

The next morning Wolf started out. Iron-Man's house was in the middle of the sea. When Wolf came nearer, the house began to shake and Wolf entered it with a breath of air. Iron-Man saw him and said, "You have arrived at your friend's dwelling." Iron-Man was trailing his long pipe along the floor. He cut his tobacco, filled his pipe and began to smoke. He handed the pipe to Wolf, who smoked up all of the tobacco. Then the father of the Indians took his little pipe from a quiver. Clouds of smoke rose. He handed the pipe to Iron-Man, but he could not smoke it all up. He filled the house with smoke until he was completely stupefied by it. Wolf's son told his father that Iron-Man was nearly dead. Then Wolf dispelled the smoke and made Iron-Man well again.

They sat down for a while. Then Iron-Man brought a large iron ball, of which he gave half to his friend. "We are now going to make guns," he said. Both made guns as quickly as possible, putting them up as soon as they were completed. Wolf made more guns in the same time than Iron-Man. The father of the Indians won.

The Sun

Long ago the Sun was so near to the earth that it burnt people to death. All the Indians said to Cottontail, "The sun is too hot. Get into a hole and shoot it from there." In the evening, Cottontail hid in a hole and stayed there until sunrise. When the Sun came up in the morning, Cottontail shot his arrows at it, but they were all burnt up. Someone told him to use his fire-drill instead of an arrow. He took the drill and shot it at the Sun. He knocked the Sun down into his hole. This is how Cottontail's neck and legs were burnt yellow.

The Sun was dead. The people cut open its chest and took out its gall. Then they talked about who should make the Sun go up. "Perhaps the Horned-Toad can make it go up with his long horns," they said. The Horned-Toad took the Sun and raised it on his horns to where it is now.

The Bear and the Deer

The Bears and the Deer were neighbors. One day the old Bear and the old Deer went to dig roots, while their children remained at home. The women sat down to delouse each other. "Let me take the lice from the back of your neck," said Bear, but instead she wrung Deer's neck. Then she returned home bringing Deer's flesh with her. "Our mother is returning," said one of the cubs, "She is bringing meat and fat." "Keep still," said the older one. "Don't show it to the Deer." They ate up the Deer's flesh. Then they said to the fawns, "This is your mother's fat." The young Deer cried when they saw what had happened. The old Bear went to them and said, "Don't cry, your mother has found many roots. She has gone to sleep and will come back again. I am going to her now." She went away to get some more meat.

The Fawns wished to avenge their mother's death, so they asked the Cubs to play with them. "Let two of us go into the sweat lodge and take a sweatbath," they said. The Cubs agreed, and the Deer went in first. When there was too much heat and steam, they cried, "Let us get out," and the Bears allowed them to go out. "Now you two go inside," the Fawns said and the Bears agreed. When the Cubs were inside, the Deer fanned smoke in. After a while the Bears asked to be let out but, instead, the Fawns stopped up every little hole as quickly as possible and the Cubs suffocated. The Deer painted the Cubs' faces red, and placed the corpses at the entrance to Bear's wikiup. When the Bear came home, she saw her children peeping out at her and noticed their appearance. "You are wasting my red paint," she said. When she realized what had happened, she ran around in a passion of grief crying, "Who has killed them? Who has killed my children?"

The Fawns said to each other, "How could we kill the Cubs?" Soon after they ran away, but after a while the younger one got tired. When he was quite exhausted, they took refuge in a pine trunk and went to sleep in the hollow of the tree. However, the old Bear had tracked them and came up to their resting-place. The older Fawn saw her coming and woke up his brother. "Here is the one who wishes to eat us up, she has overtaken us. Come, wake up, younger brother." The Bear did not wish to eat them in the dark. "At daybreak," she said to herself, "I shall make a good feast of them." She was so tired she went to sleep and slept soundly. The two young ones got out of the tree, jumped over her and ran away.

They arrived at the bank of the Salmon River. Their maternal grandfather was sitting there with his legs stretched out. "Ho! Take us across, Blue-Bald-Head (a bird)." He allowed them to pass over his legs to the other side of the stream. They ran to their grandfather's lodge and the old man transformed them into Deer.

The Bear thought of the feast she would have as she tracked the children. She came to the river and asked Blue-Bald Head to let her cross. He stretched out his legs and the old woman went across. When she got to his knee, she bent down to drink and hit his knee with her cup. He pulled up his legs and the Bear fell into the water. She did not pursue the Deer any more. She floated for a month and came out where her Cubs had been killed. When she looked at her body, she saw that all the hair had come off.

Dzo'avits and the Weasels

Weasel was living in his lodge. In the evening, he began to long for his brother. He grew sleepy and his wife told him to go to bed, but he still thought of his older brother. "A giant is eating my older brother," he said. He cried and continued to cry all night. His wife asked him to keep still but he did not cease wailing. "My brother is being eaten by the giant, Dzo'avits." At last he fell asleep, but he began to cry again when he woke up in the morning. His wife said, "Keep quiet! Perhaps your brother will be back soon."

Weasel, however, went away crying. He knew where the giant's tent was situated, so he went to it and looked in. He had his obsidian knife with him. A woman was sitting there, weaving a willow cup. Weasel entered and sat down. He saw a large knife covered with blood hanging in the lodge. "Let me have that cup," said Weasel to the woman. She cleaned the bottom of the cup and then gave it to him. Weasel hung the cup around his neck, even though it was very greasy. He sat down and remained seated for a long time. At last he heard the giant coming home. The giant dropped his bundle outside and entered the lodge.

As soon as he came in, he told the woman to prepare some food. "I have brought some Indians home." The wife arose, took the large, bloody knife and went outside where her husband had left his Indian captives, but she could not find any in his bag. "There are none here," she said. "You must have lost them. Where are they?" "There are not many of them," the giant answered. "There are only a few. They may be in the bottom of

150

the bag." He looked in, but the Indians were gone. He began to cry. At last he stopped crying and sat down.

He looked at Weasel and noticed that he was very fat, so the giant thought he would be good to eat. He proposed that they should try to cut each other's throats. Weasel agreed and the giant took his big knife. "I'll try to cut yours first," said Weasel. The giant put his head in position and Weasel tried to cut his neck. The giant laughed and said to his wife, "You must not look at us two." The woman lay down and covered herself up. The giant again told her she must not watch them.

Weasel began to cut once more, then he drew out his obsidian knife. He was going to use it and the woman noticed it. "What kind of a stone has that boy got? What is the boy doing there?" she asked. The giant pulled away. "Where is that knife?" "Nowhere," said Weasel. "I spat it out, I threw it away. I don't have it any more." Then he began to cut the giant's neck. Dzo'avits again warned his wife not to watch them, so she lay down and covered her face. Weasel placed his knife against the giant's throat and the giant fell asleep. Then Weasel took out his obsidian and cut off the giant's head. He carried it outside and threw it away. The woman arose and the boy struck her with the knife and killed her. Thus he killed them both.

Then Weasel sat down and wept for a long time. Finally, he stopped, picked up the head of an Indian, looked at it and threw it away again. He could not find his older brother's gray hair, though he searched for it everywhere. He picked up one Indian head after another, but could not find his brother's gray hair. He sat down and cried for a long time. At last he picked up the giant's head. Then he examined the giant's body. At last he pulled off the giant's teeth and looked between his jaws. There between the giant's big teeth, he found his brother's gray hair. He took it out and in the night he brought it home crying.

At home he tied it to his fire-drill and stuck it in the ground until morning. His wife was there. In the morning, his brother came to life and called Weasel, "Get up, younger brother." Weasel said, "My older brother is talking, listen to him." The older brother said, "Get up and eat." Weasel looked at his brother, threw his arms about him and kissed him. "Let me alone and eat," said the older brother. Both of them laughed.

The older brother was well again, but he could not lie down comfortably.

The Weasel Brothers

A giant was walking and pulling along some wood. Weasel tracked him until he caught sight of him. When Weasel got close enough, he hit the giant. "What is this?" asked the giant. "That boy has hit me." They built a fire, and the giant proposed a wrestling-match. "Whoever loses shall be thrown into the fire." Weasel won and, throwing his opponent into the fire, killed him with a fire-stick.

Then Weasel started off toward the giant's lodge. "Take care," said Weasel's older brother. "Another powerful giant will kill you. Don't go over there." Weasel was not afraid, and did not believe what his brother told him. As he was going along, he saw another giant looking down from a cliff. Weasel hit that giant, too, making him bark like a dog. "What is that?" he shouted. "That Weasel has struck me." Then the giant tried to trick Weasel. "Come, younger brother," he cried, "look down at these girls." When Weasel approached him, the giant tried to hurl him down, but Weasel evaded him, and stole up behind him. The giant looked down. "Have I killed him?" he asked. Weasel, who by then was standing behind the giant, pushed him over and killed him.

Weasel went on his way again. "Take care," said his brother. "Strong bear will kill you. Don't go in that direction. There is a bear with two cubs who kills strangers in a swinging-game. They will kill you immediately." "My older brother," said Weasel, "I am going to look for them." He arrived at their home. They put him down but he jumped in time and was not hurt. Then he told the bears to get into the swing. He threw them all down and killed them. He scraped off the old bear's flesh, and put on her skin. In the meantime, the old Weasel had tracked him, thinking he might have been killed by the bear. At sunrise, he caught up to him and saw the bear's tracks. He

152

peeped through the willows, took aim at the supposed bear and shot at it. He missed it by a trifle. Weasel jumped up and laughed at his brother. Then the older Weasel also laughed. "What is the matter with you? You frightened me." "Oh, it was only a joke," Weasel answered.

The older Weasel wanted to hunt water-elk. They went to the bank of the stream, and the older brother took off his clothing. "I am going into the water," he said. "I am going to hunt water-elk. You must not get frightened, because you will die of thirst if you run away." He went in further and the water came up to his eyes. At last he was entirely beneath the water. The water-elk were standing up and jumping around. The younger Weasel suddenly became frightened and ran away, shooting off his arrows.

He famished with thirst. The old Weasel had killed an elk and was skinning it. "Perhaps my younger brother ran away," he thought, "and died of thirst." He left the elk entrails in the water and tracked his brother. At last he found him, gave him water to drink, and made his younger brother wake up again.

Coyote and the Rock

Coyote was walking along a river when he came to a large white rock. Everyone was afraid of it, but Coyote walked right up to it and spat on it. Then he went away. After a while Coyote looked back and the rock seemed to be rolling after him.

Coyote thought, "That rock will never be able to catch me," so he ran along, making fun of the rock. At first he ran along the slope of a hill. The rock followed him. He went downhill again, and this time he was nearly caught. He ran through a narrow gorge, but the rock shattered the rocks in its way and continued the chase. Coyote crossed a stream. The rock plunged in and followed. Coyote went through a wood. The rock made a path for itself by knocking down all the trees.

Coyote did not know what to do. The rock was just behind him, treading on his tail and heels.

Then Coyote saw a Bear digging for wild carrots. "Aunt," he cried, "this rock is going to kill me, get behind me." The Bear stepped between them and stood up on her hind legs, but the rock knocked her to pieces. Coyote fled until he came to an Elk. "This rock is killing me," he cried. "Get behind me." The Elk got behind him, and raised his antlers against the rock, but the rock crushed him and went after Coyote.

Finally, Coyote came to a man who was building a fire. "Brother," he cried, "the rock is killing me." The man apparently paid no attention to Coyote, but when the rock approached, he just pushed out his elbow and hit it. The rock was shattered into small pieces. The man had large beads on his elbow, which formed his medicine, and it was this charm that killed the rock. Coyote fell to the ground, completely exhausted. After some time he arose, walked around the hill and killed the man by striking him with a stone. He then stole the charm and put it on his arm.

Coyote now walked uphill and got ready for a rock that might tumble down. A rock began to roll down. As it approached Coyote, he put out his elbow and it was split asunder. "This is nothing," said Coyote. He went up higher and waited for a bigger rock to tumble toward him. The rock came down, but before Coyote had time to stretch out his elbow, it crushed and killed him. Only his tail stuck out beneath.

Skunk

Eagle was Skunk's younger brother. While Eagle was away hunting, ten Frog women came to the lodge to marry Skunk, and five Rabbit women came who wanted Eagle for a husband. Skunk kept the Rabbits for himself and put the Frogs under Eagle's bed. At night Eagle returned with some deer and asked Skunk to cook the meat. After preparing the food, Skunk gave all of it to the Rabbits. Eagle asked, "What have you done with all the food?" "I have eaten it all because I was very hungry." When it got dark they went to bed. Suddenly Skunk laughed. Eagle asked, "What are you laughing at?" Skunk said, "Nothing. A mouse was running over my face." The Frogs woke up Eagle and said, "Those Rabbit women came to marry you. We are his wives." Then Eagle gave them some food and the Frogs left.

The next morning, Eagle told Skunk to prepare some food. Then Eagle proposed that they should get some game he had killed. Skunk did not believe he had killed any, but at last he agreed to go. They found some elk and Eagle said, "I forgot my gun. I'll go home to get it." Skunk went to get it for him, but Eagle said, "No, you can't run as fast as I." Then Eagle returned and found his wives under Skunk's bed. He went away with the five women and sat down on the top of a high rock.

Skunk ran home, but could not find his wives there, so he decided to kill Eagle. He looked for him everywhere and got very tired. He lay down in the shade, then grew thirsty and walked to a brook. As he looked into the water, he thought he saw Eagle and the women there, so he blew away the water. At last, he saw them on the rock and asked Eagle to give him the youngest woman. Eagle answered, "No, she is my best wife." Skunk said, "Well, brother, give me any one of them," but Eagle refused. Then Skunk asked, "How did you climb up there? Is there any way to climb to that rock?" Eagle replied, "I climbed up with my head down and my feet up." As the Skunk began to climb, Eagle hit him with a red-hot rock. Skunk fell into the water and his scent floated away.

Skunk got out alive, but he could not find his scent. He looked for it down the river and asked a woman who lived there, "Have you seen my scent?" He went down and asked all the people who lived on the banks of the river. One woman said, "Some Indians are keeping your scent over by the mountain." He walked in that direction and met Meadowlark. Skunk asked him, "Where is my scent?" The bird answered, "An orphan boy is playing with it continually. When he does not play with it, he always cries. As soon as he gets it, he is satisfied." Skunk went on until he saw the child playing with his scent. The boy was throwing it in the air and it looked like a fire in the night. Skunk watched closely, seized the scent and fled. The child cried and the Indians searched for the scent, but failed to find it.

Skunk now turned back. He met many Indians, and killed them all with his scent. Then he robbed them of their beads and their other ornaments. He walked on and met other Indians whom he killed and robbed in the same way. When he came to the next village, a wolf recognized him. Five wolves watched him when he got there. When they saw the beads that he had stolen from the dead Indians, they decided to punish him. They walked up behind him and stepped on his tail. Skunk said, "Let me alone, brothers." One wolf said, "Let us kill him." They seized his tail and toes. He cried, "Let me loose and let us fight. This is a woman's way of acting, a man would not kill another like this." But they paid no attention to what he said and killed him.

Lodge-Boy and Thrown-Away

Long ago a man and his wife were living in a grass lodge. The man always went hunting with his bow and arrows. One morning the sun informed him in a dream that a visitor would come to them, and told him how to treat his guest. The man told his wife, who was pregnant at the time, "Whenever he comes, do not touch the ground with the food you give him. Place it on his chest, when he lies down on his back." While the man was out hunting, the visitor arrived. The woman prepared food for him and set it on the ground. He did not touch it. Then she put it on his legs, but still he would not taste it. Finally, she put it on his chest and he ate it all up.

When he was through eating, the woman fell down dead. The visitor rubbed her body and took out two boys from her womb. He threw one of them into the water, so he was called Pagaruntandzauwuhe, The-One-Who-Has-Been-Thrown-into-the-Water, and he threw the other one into the entrance of the wickiup, so his name became Katazantandzauwuhe, The-One-Who-Was-Thrown-into-the-Entrance-of-the-Wickiup. Then he went away.

The Indian did not know what had happened when he came home and found his wife dead and her womb emptied. While he was preparing some food, someone cried, "Give me some food, father." He looked around, but could not see anyone. Three times the baby bobbed up crying in this way, but the hunter could not see it, because it disappeared below the grass. The fourth time he saw its face and body. It went down once more and when he reappeared, he was already a young man. His father asked, "Why don't you get up and eat?" So the boy ate.

The next morning the man made a willow hoop and gave it to his son to play with. "Don't roll it southwards," he warned. When he returned in the evening, he found the boy's face badly scratched. "Who did that?" asked the hunter. The boy told him it was his brother Pagaruntandzauwuhe that had scratched his face. The next day the hunter told his son to play in the same place as before. "If your brother comes up to scratch you, hold ⁻ him till I come."

The man hid nearby to watch. When Pagaruntandzauwuhe came out of the water, he tried to scratch Katazantandzauwuhe's face. His own face was yellow. His father seized him, bound his hands and feet, and took him to the grass lodge. There he told the boys they were brothers and should never fight. They were the first twins ever born and soon they began to look like each other.

One day while their father was out hunting, the boys cooked some food in an earthen pot. Their mother was still lying on the ground unburied. "Get up, mother, tend to the meat," said the twins. "You wake her up," said Lodge-Boy to his brother. "You are clever." He saw his mother's fingers twitching and tried to rouse her, but failed. Then Thrown-Away took a stick, put it in his mother's hand, grasped her wrist and made her stir the meat in the earthen pot. Suddenly she woke up, sat up straight and continued stirring the food. She began to eat and walk about, and looked very handsome. Her husband came home and noticed how pretty she looked.

The hunter made a new hoop for the twins. He told them not to throw it southward. When the boys were playing, they forgot about his warning and rolled the hoop toward the south. The hoop rolled without stopping. The boys ran after it throwing their sticks, but it still went on rolling. At last it got to the shore of the big sea. Lodge-Boy asked his brother to let it go, but Thrown-Away followed. The hoop fell into the water where it turned into a water buffalo. Thrown-Away ran into the monster's stomach. Lodge-Boy dug a hole near the shore and waited for the animal to come out. The next morning at sunrise, when the water buffalo went ashore, Lodge-Boy took his bow and shot the buffalo. It ran back to the sea and fell dead at the shore. The boy skinned it and cut it open. Thrown-Away came out smiling with his hoop. They cut the animal into small pieces and cooked its flesh. Then they started homeward.

They came to a strange tribe of Indians who locked travelers up in a dark rock, where they could not get out and finally died. The boys were imprisoned in the usual way. "Thrown-Away, get us out. You know something," said his brother. Pagaruntandzauwuhe began to think how they could be saved, since he was a medicine man. He wished that it would rain, and immediately it began to rain very hard. The rain cracked the rock, the boys escaped, and again turned toward their home.

Next they came to a giant. He said to them, "If you go to those willows and get sticks from them, I shall make arrows for you." The giant kept a great many bear dogs under the trees and hoped they would devour the two boys. When they saw the bear dogs under the willows, Pagaruntandzauwuhe asked his brother to take the lead. Katazantandzauwuhe said, "No, you are the clever one, you ought to go first." So Thrown-Away started out and when he got to the bears, he kicked them aside right and left, making a path for himself and his brother. At first Katazantandzauwuhe was afraid and held back, then he followed his brother's footsteps. They took the sticks from the willows and brought them to the giant, who now made arrows for them. Then they set out once more for their home.

They came to a large white rock which they cut into little pieces. They put the white fragments on the mountain tops.

That is why there is snow on the mountains today. At last they reached home. Their father was now an old man and their mother was very old also. The mother died a short time after. Two days after her death her husband died of old age. This is why people die of old age now.

The Sheep-Woman

Two brothers were living together with their wife. The older brother went out hunting every day, while the woman went in search of roots. One morning the older man found the trail of a mountain sheep and followed it around the mountainside. Toward evening it led him back toward his lodge again and he gave up the chase. His wife had returned before him and he told her how he had tracked the sheep. He decided to start again on the next day and try to catch the animal.

The next morning the woman went out digging and, after eating, her husband also left the lodge. Again he found the sheep's trail, it was a fresh track going around the mountain. Toward evening it led him back to his wickiup again. His wife was home when he returned. He told his younger brother to set out for the other side of the mountain where there were no trees and where he might be able to catch sight of the sheep. Accordingly, they started out the next morning. The woman also left in order to dig roots, but she never brought any home. She told her husband she could not get any food because of her baby which cried all the time and had to be nursed.

The younger brother stayed out for three days. He went to the summit of the mountain and was fatigued by the time he reached the top. His guardian spirit ordered him to build a big fire and he obeyed. After a while, he saw the woman coming along. The youth drew nearer and pulled his bowstring. Hearing the noise, the woman looked up, saw the man and hurried home. The baby was crying.

The young man returned to the place assigned by his brother and fell asleep. His brother came up and asked whether he had seen anything. The youth had forgotten all about the woman and said he had not seen anything because he had been asleep all the time. The older brother began to upbraid him. "Why didn't you watch? I told you to watch." Then the youth recollected and informed his brother of what he had seen. They went home. When they arrived there, they found the woman busy. "Why don't you bring any roots home?" they asked her. She said the child had kept her busy again, but she would leave it home the next time.

The brothers decided to play a trick on her. They turned themselves into mountain sheep and stood on the creek near their lodge. The little boy was with them. In the evening the woman came home, and seeing the sheep so near their dwelling, she thought the men must have fallen asleep. "You sleepy heads, there are some sheep right out here. Get up!" When no one got up, she went in, took a bow and arrow and shot at them herself, but the sheep ran away. The woman pursued them, but whenever she came up to them, they managed to escape. They went far across the mountains and the woman continued to follow them.

At last, their wife got to Coyote's people. She informed Coyote of the big sheep that had run away there. Coyote painted himself up and announced the news to his fellow tribesmen. The Indians scattered to hunt down the game, but failed to catch them. At last Red Grasshopper went out. He saw the sheep running toward him, tore off a patch from his moccasins, pasted it on his forehead to disguise himself, and then shot the baby sheep. The other Indians hunted other game.

When they returned to camp, the woman sharpened a stick and tested the hide of each animal brought in. When she struck Grasshopper's sheepskin, the stick broke in two immediately. Accordingly, she married Grasshopper. Coyote was jealous. "A man must have a loose jointed leg like Grasshopper's," he said. "Then one can get a girl easily. If I had a leg like that, I would have won the woman."

The Bear's Son

Bear killed his father and then his mother married a White man, who sent the boy to school. The White children teased the Bear child. They made fun of his long nose and whipped him, so the Bear boy went to the blacksmith's shop and had an iron pole made there. Eight steers were not strong enough to pull it to pieces. Bear went home and told his mother he was going out alone to hunt the enemy, but he went to school first. The White children began to make fun of him again. "Your nose is big," they said. "Don't come in here." Bear took his rod and killed all the White children with it, then he went far away.

He saw an Indian who was moving dirt. The Indian asked him, "Where are you going?" "I'm looking for the enemy." "I think I will go along with you," said the man. "Two of us will not be afraid of anything." They went along until they met another Indian who was moving rocks from one place to another. "Where are you two going?" he asked. "We are going far away to look for the enemy." "Let us three go together, and we'll not be afraid of anything we may see." They went along until they saw an Indian who was transplanting a pine. The Indian asked what they were doing and joined them saying, "Four of us will not be afraid of anything."

They went along until they came to a creek with willow trees on its banks, and they entered a house there. "Tomorrow," they said, "three of us will go hunting and Earth-Mover will stay home and cook." The next morning the three others went out to hunt, and Earth-Mover cooked. When he was done, he looked at a newspaper. Suddenly Iron-Head-Man came in and asked for some food, but Earth-Mover refused. Iron-Head-Man pulled him about, knocked him down, and ate up all the food. Then he went away.

In the evening the hunters came home laughing. They asked Earth-Mover why he had not prepared any food. He answered that he had wanted to cook, but had fallen down in reaching

161

for some food that was kept near the top of the house. The next day Rock-Mover stayed at home to cook. Again Iron-Head came in, knocked him down and disappeared after eating all the food. When the hunters came back, Rock-Mover gave the same excuse for not having any food for them. On the following day, Pine-Transplanter met with the same adventure.

Finally, Bear stayed at home. When he was through with his work, he began to whistle and to walk back and forth with his rod. He knew that Iron-Head was the ghost of his older brother. Iron-Head came and asked for food, but Bear refused. They wrestled, and Bear killed the ghost by throwing him and cutting his throat. The head jumped away by itself and went down into a hole.

The hunters, coming home in the evening, laughed when they saw there was plenty of food. They thought Iron-Head had not come that day and would not believe that the boy had killed him. Bear took them to the hole and showed them the blood around its edge. Then he told them to bring a rope.

The men brought Bear a large rope and tied a bell to it. They were to be let down into the hole, one by one. As soon as any one rang the bell, it would mean that he was frightened and the others were to pull him up. Rock-Mover, Earth-Mover, and Pine-Transplanter went in one after the other. Then one after the other they each rang the bell and were pulled up again. Then Bear went down, met three men, killed them and took their wives, whom he hoisted up on the ropes.

When the first woman came out of the hole, Earth-Mover said, "I'll take you for a wife." Pine-Transplanter and Rock-Mover married the other women. Then the men cut the rope and Bear fell down and broke his limbs. His older brother picked him up and healed his wounds. Then Bear asked his brother which was the swiftest animal and his brother told him the eagle was. They gave the eagle three sheep to eat, then Bear mounted him and flew up on his back. They flew faster and faster. Bear cut off some of his own flesh to feed the eagle so as to make him fly still faster, but although Bear tracked the Indians who had stolen his wives, he never found them.

Northern Paiute Myths

The Creation of the Indian

Coyote's children were playing the hand game indoors. A woman outside warned them, "Boys, listen, something is coming." However, they paid no attention to her. She said again, "Boys, an ogre is coming." Still they paid no attention to her. Her husband was inside and she asked him to keep her child there while she jumped into a pit and covered it up. The ogre came and killed all of the boys. Then he said, "I have killed them all." The woman heard him say this. He sang as he went away.

She crawled out of the pit about sunrise and heard her boy crying indoors. "You had better come to me, my child," she said. She stretched out her hand and he took it and came out. They found some food growing on the mountains and the woman dug it up and ate. She made the child sleep there, then left him. A second ogre met her and asked, "Where is your home?" She replied, "Over there on that knoll. A man like you is there." She was pointing out the place where her boy was.

The ogre went there and swallowed him but wanted more to eat, so he returned for the woman. When she saw him coming back, she dug a hole and crawled into it. The ogre tracked her all over but failed to find her. At last he scraped away the earth with his hand and almost uncovered her hiding place, but just before he got to her he said, "It is nearly sunset time. I'll stop now and get her tomorrow." The woman knew that in a little more time he would have unearthed her. She was crying for he would have swallowed her.

She got out and ran away. The ogre came the next day and continued digging, but he only found the empty hole. Meanwhile, the woman met an old woman who said, "You can hide there, but I don't know what to do with you. My grandchildren are no good. They will eat you up when they get home." The old woman dug a hole before her grandchildren's return, put the woman in it and covered the opening with willows.

One grandchild came and said, "Coming here I saw someone's tracks." "I have not seen anyone today," the old woman answered. "Well, I saw tracks there," "I was over there, I think you saw my tracks," said the old woman. The rest of the grandchildren came carrying cottontails, birds, and other food. They cooked the food, but the old woman did not eat. "Why don't you eat?" they asked. "I'll eat tomorrow. Tomorrow I shall not have any food, so I am leaving it till then." The hidden woman watched them through the willow covering. All the grandchildren were lying around the fire without their blankets.

Before sunrise they went hunting and then the old woman said to her guest, "You had better get up and go. Eat what I have here and go to your destination. There are many dangerous things on the road and you had better not touch them when you pass by. There are heads by the road. Don't touch any head on the road or it will hurt you." The woman went on and found the heads just like the old woman said. She touched one head, and it began to pursue her. She became frightened and ran on as fast as she could.

She arrived at a camp where a man asked her, "Well, have you touched a head on the road?" "Yes, one on this side," she replied. "Then it is coming," the man said and shut up his house. He stuck some sticks on the roof and told the woman to sit down under them. They heard the head coming before they saw it. It struck the ground as it came along and bounced backward and forward. When it tried to climb up after the woman, the sticks got stuck in the orbits of its eyes and the head stayed there. The man went outside, looked at it, took it down and gave it to the woman saying, "Take this head back to where it belongs and put it back exactly like it was before." She did as he said. Then he told her, "If you wish to go, go. There are two camps on the road. The people of the first camp eat nothing, but those of the second eat all kinds of fruit."

The woman arrived at the first house and its owner said, "I eat bad food that is not suitable for you. Find another man on the road and stay with him." At the second house a man asked her, "Where do you come from?" "From over there," she said. "Tell me all about it. Then I'll give you something to eat." She told him she was looking for a certain man and he gave her food. She was close to her destination and the man told her, "You have only a short distance to go. From the summit you can see the house you are looking for."

She went to that house and that is how she got to Job's peak. There was plenty to eat there, so she picked up some food and ate it sitting outside on the south side of the house. The owner of the house said, "There is enough to eat here. Come in and sew my moccasins." She opened the door and entered. The man sat on one side of the house and she on the other. He prepared some food and gave it to her. When she had eaten, she went outdoors and gave the man some of her food. He ate some and returned the remainder to her. And so they were married.

The next day the man went hunting and in the evening he returned with an antelope. On his way home he saw a boy and a girl who said, "Our father has got something to eat." The next day he went hunting again. When he came back home, he saw two more children. The boys and girls ran up to him saying, "Our father seems to have something to eat." In this way he made four children in two days. The man and woman were the Paviotso.

The boys always shot at each other under their father's legs and the girls also fought. When they grew up, they made arrow points and used them in their fights. Their father said, "Don't do that, you are brothers," but the boys paid no attention to him. "If you don't stop fighting, I'll send you to different places and I'll go elsewhere myself, and then people will only be able to come to me when they die. If you don't stop, I'll send one pair of you to Stillwater and the other to Lovelocks." The boys went down to the valley and returned before sunset, but one was bleeding because he had been hurt by the other's arrow. The father lost all patience and sent one pair to Stillwater and the other to Lovelocks saying, "Now if you want to continue fighting, keep on as long as you wish."

One boy and one girl went to Stillwater Valley and made a fire with a light smoke. In Lovelocks the smoke was darker. The father saw it and after a while he began to go that way by walking under the rocks. He and his wife were crying because they felt sorry for the children. The man cried aloud and broke a rock making a cleft that is still visible east of Job's Peak. They were crying and their marks are still to be seen, because their tears turned into springs. Where there was plenty of water the father took out his bow and arrows and shot at the rocks, and the arrows are still on the rock. He made Chalk Mountain there.

On the other side, at Westgate, they camped and cried, making another spring. At Middlegate he said, "My children, whenever you come for pine-nuts, come here and drink this water." They went on farther and got to Eastgate and he made a big rock there. "Whenever my boys come here, let them rub their foreheads against those rocks." He went on and camped on the other side of Eastgate. The impression of his feet can be seen by the springs on the north side. On the other side there was another spring and there he piled up some rocks. "Whenever my boys suffer from disease, let them come here and give beads to the rock and ask it to cure them."

His wife, said, "Which way are you going? We'll never find a better place. We might as well go back to our boys, I am sorry for them." The man said, "Don't say that. We might find a better country." He went on and then stopped. The woman said, "I'd like to go back to our boys." He answered, "We are pretty near our destination. We'll get there soon."

He came to a body of water and walked over to it as though it were land. On the other side he found a white mountain where he stopped and sat down for a while. The woman did not say a word. Farther on he found a spot and while sitting there, he opened the clouds and told his wife to look through. "Perhaps you will find another country." She looked and saw a beautiful valley which was green all over. He said, "I think we had better go through the clouds to the beautiful country. Don't grieve too much. Perhaps some day the boys will die and come to us. Whenever anyone dies, he'll come to us." They went there but no mountain was to be seen there at all except in the east, where there was only a little one. "We ought to go and find some timber so that we can live under it." They looked until they found some and then they made camp there.

The man went hunting as before and they lived very well.

One day he went to the little mountain and found seed there like ours. He told his wife, "This is our fruit. You had better get some so we can live on it. Be careful if you go to the mountain every day, or our children may catch some disease and die. Then they may come here and you may find them."

Once she found something that looked as if it had been used. When her husband returned from the hunt she gave him some food and told him about her find. "It looks like fire," she said and showed it to him. He said, "This might come from our old home. I don't know what to do with it." He pulled it back. "We might spoil it, but we'll know pretty soon. Perhaps our children are coming back this way. If people die and we do our part, they will come here." They did not know what do and were crying, when the woman looked round and saw somebody far off.

She did not tell her husband immediately, but sat down. Soon after this she rose and looked again and saw that it looked like someone moving. Then she told the man, "It looks like somebody is coming." "Well, it may be some people," he said. "There was no one living before we came here. Be quiet." She looked again. "It looks like a person." The man said, "Long ago I saw one person here, maybe he has come back." The woman looked again and saw that it was a person. Her husband said, "You had better prepare food for him. He may be hungry."

He arrived and the man knew who he was. The man said to his wife, "Perhaps you know what we are going to do. He comes from your old home." The stranger said, "I thought you were no better than I. You had better fix it properly so that dying persons may come here. Make some basket-jugs, one big one and one small one, and put your find in there. See what will happen." The woman obeyed, put some water in the jugs, and threw in their find. They found little babies in the water. "Keep them in there a while," the stranger said.

They looked again, and one child was already old enough to walk. They washed it with water. "Take the children to the little mountain," said the newcomer. "Let them go through one hole the first time, then they will grow a little more. Let them come through the second hole, then they will be of the same age as you." They gave them something to eat and then they sent them out. As they left the man said, "There is a good place for you and there you have to be, go and stay there. Perhaps more will come and I'll send them over to you."

The Theft of the Pine-Nuts

Coyote and Wolf were brothers who lived in the eastern Pine-Nut Range. Squirrels, cottontails, the Crow, and all the four-footed animals lived there. One day when they were playing the hand game, the Crow began to feel as if he were being strangled by something that smelled peculiar. All of them began to wonder what it could be. Coyote got up to see where the odor came from. First he went south, then west, then east. When he turned north, he found where the smell had come from. It was late in the afternoon and he said, "I'll see what it is." He started out saying, "Let my steps be made into miles, so I can get there quickly."

He made the trip in a short time and soon arrived where the other tribe was living. They were the Crane people. He sat down and watched them and when the little ones passed with pine-nuts in their hands, he tried to jar their hands so he could get some. Crane was chief. He was suspicious of Coyote so he made a speech to his people, telling them not to make the pine-nut mush as thick as usual, but to make it very thin. They did so and gave some to Coyote. When they gave him a cupful of soup, he wanted to take it home, but he did not know how. He put some into his mouth, but then he swallowed it. Then he tried to put some in his coyote robe, but it was so thin, the soup ran through and could not be held. "I cannot take any home," he thought, "but I'll run home and tell them about it. Let my steps be made into miles, so I may get home soon."

Coyote got home and told his brothers what a fine meal he had had with his brothers from afar and that he had found the food detected by the Crow. Wolf then made a speech telling the people of Coyote's find and told all the animals to get ready to go and get some of the food Coyote had found. Everyone went with Coyote and Wolf except Hummingbird who said, "I'll stay home and keep the place. I'll watch for you and when I see you returning I'll make a big fire and smoke."

While on their way they had to hunt deer to live on. They travelled all day and stopped at night, but they had no water. All of them were pretty thirsty and said, "What shall we do without water tonight? Somebody ought to get us some." They talked it over and decided that Coyote should get the water, and he was to get all the marrow from the deer bones as his reward when he got back.

Coyote went for water. While he was gone, the rest said he was getting too much pay for his work and that someone with a sharp bill ought to remove the marrow from some of the bones. Then they would pile the good bones on top so that Coyote might not notice the deception at first. Crow said, "I'll do it." So he took the marrow out of about half the bones, then they piled the bad ones under the good ones. When Coyote got back, everyone hurried to get a drink of water before he should find out. While he was eating the good bones on top, they quickly drank the water. When he got to the empty ones, he broke one bone after another, but found no marrow. He became angry and was going to empty the water, but all the people had had their drink. The people gave him a little fat then, but Lizard came along and fell into it while it was boiling. Lizard did not get hurt, but Coyote was so angry he chased Lizard, who ran into the river. Coyote could not follow him there, so he said, "Your name will be Fish from now on, not Lizard. The Lizards outside the water shall be black."

Crane's people were suspicious when they saw Coyote's people coming from afar, so they made a canyon on the road and covered it with slippery ice so that Coyote's people could not pass. The next morning Coyote's people reached this canyon. Coyote was going to show the other people what he could do and scratched the ice, but that did not help. The Crows were there and Coyote said to them, "How do you think you will get across, you black things? I am a mighty man, but still I cannot pass." Coyote made fun of them and one of the Crows said, "We'll show him that we are mightier than he is.

One of us will fly so high and come down so hard that he will crack the ice." Another Crow said, "I'll go up the second time and come down so as to break it in so many pieces that each one will be able to pass."

So one Crow flew high up and roared like the thunder. Coyote looked up and said, "There is nothing up there, only a little red cloud." The Crow came down so that the ice cracked with a terrible thud. Then the second Crow went up and came down with still greater force, breaking the ice all up so that the people could pass through. Now Coyote said, "It is a very good thing you have done my sister's son, but I'll be the first one to pass." But he had on his back such a load of wild flax for netting that he got caught in the narrow passage and could not get through. So everyone jostled him and got ahead of him, and he was the last to go through.

At last they got to Crane's people. When they got there, the first thing they did was play a hand game. They began to play and continued till morning. The Cranes were winning, but then Crow got into the game and his side began to win. Crow was a very handsome man. He wore a pebble necklace, and today his neck is still very pretty. While this gambling was going on, the Mice were looking for the pine-nuts, which the Cranes had hidden in a tree trunk so that none of the large animals could find them. The Mice looked everywhere without finding what they sought. At last one of them ran to the top of a tree, and at the top there was an old bow, and in the middle of the bow there was a pine-nut.

Just at daybreak the Mice reported they had found the nut. When Coyote heard of it he said, "I'll make them all sleep, and we'll take the pine-nut home with us." However, the nut was hidden so high that nothing but a bird could get it. They said to the Woodpeckers, "You go and break the tree in two and take out the nut." Woodpecker said, "Our bills are not strong enough." Another Woodpecker said, "We'll put our two bills together, then they'll be strong enough." So they put the two bills together and one of them flew up with a long bill and broke the tree. When he got the nut out, he set out straight for home. Wolf said, "You all go first and I'll follow in the rear."

When Crane awoke and found that the nut was taken he

made a speech. "We are starving. If there's an orphan here, you had better kill him and eat him, and then we'll be able to chase those people with the nut." Crane's people did so and then gave chase. They overtook the Wolf's people. First they killed Wolf and cut him all up, but could not find the nut in him. They killed one after another and searched for the nut in their bodies.

Coyote was among the foremost and he said to his companions who carried the nut, "Give me the nut, nephew, I can run very fast." But the others said, "No, don't give it to him, or he'll swallow it." Then Coyote was killed and only Crow and Chickenhawk were left. After a while no one was left but Chickenhawk. He looked back and saw that all the rest were killed so he said, "May my thigh be inflamed. Then I'll put the nut in this bad spot and they won't find it." They caught him and were going to kill him, but his odor was so bad that they took him by the neck and threw him away thinking, "The nut would not taste well if it were in him." So they turned back to the rest of his party and examined each one. "Well, our nut is gone. I suppose that stinking one has it."

Chickenhawk by this time was pretty far on his way back. When Wolf saw that the Cranes were gone, he revived and restored all the other people to life. Then they returned to their own country. Wolf and Coyote took the nut, took a bite of it, and sprinkled it all over the mountains, so that pine-nut trees should grow there. Wolf said to Coyote, "Don't swallow any of it, lest juniper trees be mingled with the nut trees. We want them all to be nut trees." But Coyote swallowed some. When he sprinkled the mountains, they were half covered with junipers and half with pine-nuts. There were only pine-nut trees where Wolf sprinkled.

When Crane came back he spoke to the people. "I don't know what we'll do. The trees are here, but there are no cones. I am going to follow them. I will not stay here, but I'll share my food with those people." He started and crossed the mountains. Looking this way he saw smoke all along the mountains, where they were cooking nuts. When Crane saw the smoke he said, "I am going right over there." When they saw him coming, they said, "Place all the rotten ones in one place and tell him to sit there and help himself." He came, sat down and helped himself, but the food was rotten. They did this because his bill was so long that they were afraid he would not leave anything for the other birds. Bluejay picked out some good nuts for Crane and gave them to him, but as soon as he touched them, they turned into rotten ones.

Crane said, "You live here in the mountains on food taken from us. I'll go to the valley and live on moss and seeds." When he said this, he began to fly. An old woman got a stick and hit him, knocking his tail off. When he saw that he had no tail, he took the ends of his feet and made a little tail for himself. He went to the valley. This is why he never goes to the mountains any more.

Cottontail and the Sun

Cottontail was once like an Indian and hunted cottontail rabbits. The days were pretty short then. Cottontail said, "I go after cottontails but can't get any because the sun goes down too soon." He became angry with the sun and said, "I'll go after him, he ought to make the day longer." Cottontail then went to his maternal grandmother and said, "I am angry at the sun, I wish you'd put up a lunch for me. I do not care who gets in my way. I'll kill them." His grandmother prepared food, and he took it along, as well as all of his arrows.

The first one he saw was a squirrel who lived with all his family on a mountain. As Cottontail was coming along, the squirrel said, "What is coming along the road there? It does not look like a man. I don't know what it is." Cottontail became angry, so he took an arrow and shot it at the squirrels. The squirrel family went into their house. Cottontail ran after them and said, "When you said that you made me angry, so I am going to kill you." So he killed every one of them.

The North Wind used to be a person. Cottontail arrived at his house when they were all away hunting cottontails. Cottontail went in and lay down. When he heard someone coming, he reddended his eyelids and the face around the eyes. Then he picked up some rocks and hung them up inside the door. Next he went to the rear and lay down watching the entrance. He thought to himself, "When the first one comes in, I'll see what I can do. Perhaps the rock will strike his forehead."

The North Wind and his family had twisted cottontail rabbit skins and stretched them about the house. When the first one came in, Cottontail was lying down without looking at him. Then he glanced up with his reddened eyes and so frightened the one coming in, that he ran back without noticing the rocks which struck and nearly broke his head. A second man came and asked, "What is inside? I'll look." He looked in, but was also frightened at Cottontail's appearance, ran out, and bumped his head against the rocks. One after another they struck their heads this way.

At last North Wind himself said, "I don't know what is inside, but ought to find out." Then one of them said, "Perhaps it is Cottontail." Then one of them addressed Cottontail, "My grandson Cottontail, I have some cottontail skins already prepared inside there, you may have them." Another one said, "I also have some, you may have them, too." Others also gave him their skins. Cottontail rejoiced at these gifts. He rose, took down all the stretched skins and put them down by his seat. Then he took down the rocks from the door and threw them away. Now everyone in the North Wind's party came in. One sat by the door, and the rest passed him and took seats one after another. There were so many people coming in that Cottontail was obliged to shift his place from the rear to the door.

The hunters skinned the game and began to bake it in a pit covered with dirt, with a fire on the top. One of them asked, "What is the matter? Aren't you going to give any to your grandchild?" They cooked only one for Cottontail and when they took the food out of the pit they gave him the poorest one. North Wind and the rest had the fat ones. They began to eat, but when they opened their rabbits, there was no fat in them. Cottontail, at last, opened his and began to smack his lips. They looked and saw that his rabbit was all fat inside. One of them said, "Let us take it away from him." So all went and seized him, but he evaded them, jumping underneath them over to the opposite side. They were piled on top of one another, and he laughed at them from the opposite side. Then he got angry. "I had better kill you," he said. So he killed them all except one young one, whom he could not find. He looked for him all over, but could not find him. At last he gave up the search and said, "Well, you are the youngest, you will be the North Wind." He took the arrows belonging to the people he had slain and went on.

Cottontail then went to a lodge where Raven and his son were living. Cottontail remained standing outside. Raven was making a noise inside sharpening his claws. Cottontail overheard him say, "Cottontail has come from the west and I hear he has killed everything on this road. When he comes here, I'll do this with my claws and kill him." Cottontail entered his house. "I heard you talking, Raven. What were you saying? Tell me." "I was only sharpening my claws. I was not saying anything." "Well, I heard you say something." "No, I was not saying anything." Still Cottontail continued asking and at last Raven said, "Well, since you keep on asking, I shall have to tell you. I was saying, 'I heard someone is coming from the west and has killed everything on this road. When he gets here, I'll sharpen my claws and stick them in his head.'" Cottontail said, "I thought you were saying that. I heard you."

Raven arranged the beds. "You may sleep on the other side of my boy's bed." "No, I should like to sleep between you two." "Very well, you may sleep between us." After the three had gone to bed, Cottontail began to snore as though sound asleep and soon old Raven was sound asleep. Then Cottontail got up and exchanged places with Raven's son. He did not fall asleep at all, but watched Raven. He had seen him stretching out his claws and that is why he changed his bed. Now the old Raven stretched out his claws and killed his own son. Then Cottontail laughed quietly, but Raven was soon asleep again.

In the morning Cottontail got up first and built a fire. Old Raven got up and saw his son was still asleep. He said, "Don't sleep all day, my son, get up. Well, sometimes the boy sleeps longer than usual." Cottontail said, "Let us play a game before breakfast." He suggested all kinds of games, but Raven would have none of them. At last he suggested an arrow game. Cottontail said, "You shoot first. I'll go up that tree and you see if you can hit me." He went off to the tree, climbed up, and sat in a crotch. But he only put his skin in the crotch and left his real body behind.

Raven began shooting at him, but the arrows only pierced the skin and left Cottontail unhurt. After Raven shot all his arrows, Cottontail put on his skin again and jumped down. He took his arrows and now Raven sat down on the crotch. Cottontail said, "You are a better shot than I. I don't think I'll be able to hit you. I'll miss every time. I have never used an arrow before." He began to shoot and missed Raven. He missed him again and again. He kept on saying all the time, "I don't think I'll be able to shoot you." At last he had only one arrow left. Cottontail raised it, straightened it, and said, "Well, here is the last one. I don't suppose I'll hit you." He shot it and Raven fell crying from his limb and died, for he was shot through the heart.

Cottontail went on to a gap in the mountains. He heard someone playing on the other side and saw someone running back and forth. It was Louse. He had arrows and was shouting, "I hear someone coming from the west, and I can kill him when he comes this way." Cottontail went up and sat down beside him. He said, "I heard you shouting. What were you saying?" "I was not saying anything." But Cottontail kept on asking the same question and at last Louse answered, "I was saying, 'Someone is coming from the west, when he comes, I'll kill him.' "

Louse had a big belly. Cottontail picked up some sagebrush bark, broke it, and crumpled it into a ball while Louse talked. Then he threw it at Louse's belly and it burst. He went on a little ways and listened. He heard Louse saying, "Well, Cottontail, you thought you'd kill me, but you can never kill me by splitting my belly. If you mashed my legs and head and the whole of my body, then you'd be able to kill me." Cottontail went back and mashed him all to pieces, but he could not find his toes. At last he said, "You do not amount to anything. You will always be a louse, so I'll let you go." Cottontail took all of Louse's arrows and other property and went on. This was the last person he met on his way to the sun.

He walked all night and by daybreak was almost there. He went a little closer and sat down on a mountain. The sun came up the mountain and when he got nearer, Cottontail shot at him, but the arrow was burnt up and it fell down. Cottontail discharged one arrow after another, but as soon as it got close to the sun it burned and fell to the ground. At last he had only his fire-drill left. This he discharged. Half of it burned up, but the rest of it hit the sun and knocked him to the ground. Cottontail ran up to him, cut open his body, took out the gall bladder and threw it straight up into the air. The sun used to go round close to the ground. Now Cottontail said, "Go straight up. Now, sun, you will shine a little longer. Then when I hunt rabbits, I'll have a longer day. Now I do not have time enough to hunt because the days are too short." Then he went back home.

After he had gone a short distance, everything began to burn behind him. The fire nearly overtook him, but he went into a badger hole and stayed there for a little while. The ground was burning and the fire got to the top of the badger hole. Ashes fell on the back of Cottontail's neck. That is why patches may now be seen on cottontails. He got out of the hole and ran a short distance. Then he found another hole between some rocks. The fire was again catching up to him and some of it caught him on the sides of his body. That is why cottontails' sides are red. He got out of the hole, and the fire was right behind him. He got into the hollow of an old tree stump. The fire spread to the tree and ashes again fell on the back of his neck, where he had been burnt before. He got under some cactus. There the fire did not bother him. The spines burnt, but the rest of the cactus did not burn, and the fire ceased there.

Cottontail came home to his grandmother. He hunted cottontails again, and the day was longer than before. He was glad of it. Once his grandmother said, "Husband." He overheard her and asked, "What are you saying?" She said, "I was not saying anything, I was only coughing." "No, you were saying something." He persisted in asking the question and at length she answered, "I said you were my husband." Thereafter he regarded his grandmother as his wife.

Centipede

Centipede was a great gambler who played the hand game and football. A large tribe lived in the valley near Centipede and men and women would go to play with Centipede, but none came back. The members of the tribe decreased until only two girls and a baby boy were left. They cried for their relatives to come back. They climbed a tree but could not see their people. They nearly starved.

The boy grew up and when he was big enough to kill small game, the girls made him a bow and arrows and told him what animals he should kill. He went out, stayed for a whole day, and returned with a lizard. The girls said, "Well, brother, this is not good to eat." "All right, grind me some seed. Tomorrow I'll go again." The next day he went off and came back with a snake. The sisters told him that was not good to eat either. "Very well, grind me some seed. I'll hunt again." But every time he brought either a snake or a lizard. One night, at last, he brought a little bird. The girls thought this was fine. "Oh, that's good. We shall cook it and divide it." So the boy thought he had done a great thing. He said, "I'll get up earlier tomorrow so that I can get another bird."

So the next day he started early and caught sight of a little bird on a bush. It did not try to get away, but when he aimed, it flew to the other side of the bush. At last it spoke to the boy, "Little boy, why do you want to kill me? If you do not kill me, I'll tell you something great. Do you know where all your people have gone?" Still the boy was going to shoot, but the bird spoke again, "No, don't shoot me. I'll make a great man of you." Then the boy stopped and listened. "Little boy, far across the mountain there lives a very bad man. He has killed all your people, cut out their hearts and dried them in his lodge. He has hung up their hands, all together, and has burnt the rest of their bodies. You can bring all your people back to life if you listen and do as I tell you." The boy fell on his knees and said, "Little bird, I'll listen."

The bird told him, "Get up before sunrise and come here to my nest." He then flew to his two eggs and said, "Come here before sunrise. These are my eggs. Just as you see the rays of the sun, my eggs will begin to wobble. Hit my eggs, and then there will be little birds under you which will take you through the sky above Centipede. He will not see you. Every morning when the sun gets high, Centipede practices. When you get above him, spit on his forehead. Tomorrow morning, come again and I'll tell you what his place looks like. He always spreads out a big red robe, but don't sit on it."

The boy came home without any game. His sisters asked, "Where is your game?" "I haven't any." They asked, "What shall we eat?" "Never mind," he replied, "we'll soon have our fill." They asked if they should prepare something for him to eat the next day but he said, "Never mind about food. I'll leave very early."

When he got up that day he was a handsome man. He went to the nest again. The bird said, "When you cross the mountain, you'll be able to see him. If he sees you, he will shake his red robe and spread it, but do not sit on it. Sit on the ground. Don't let him touch you. He will try to get his arms under yours. Choose the game you want to play, you'll beat him in the end. Don't play the hand game, but choose football. You will have to go through a dark place where it is always night. That is where the Indians lost their ball and so lost the game. After that he burned them. Those two eggs of mine shall go with you, but Centipede will not see them. One will be Gopher, the other Owl. Owl will sit on the right side in the dark place and blink his eyes so it will be light. Gopher will be on the other side. He will dig a hole and Centipede will lose his ball in it. When you have beaten him, he'll want to pay you in hearts and hands, but don't take them. Take him by the arm and burn him up. There is just one of your people left, but he is so burnt that he has turned into a Crow."

The boy struck the eggs and went flying through the air. He landed on top of a mountain. He saw Centipede shaking his red blanket. Gopher and Owl were with the boy, but the boy could not see them though he heard them talking. Centipede washed and brushed himself and said, "What a handsome man is coming." When the boy arrived, Centipede asked him to sit down on the blanket, but the boy sat on the ground instead. Centipede asked, "Why is it that you do not want to sit on my blanket?" He went inside his wickiup and got his hand game sticks, but the boy said, "No, I came to play football." "All right, whatever you wish." Centipede got ready, went into his lodge and brought two balls. "Choose your ball." The boy chose the right one and they went to the starting place. Both began to run. When he got to the dark place, the boy did not know where he was, but Owl blinked his eyes so that he could see his ball. He got out, carried it to the goal and was bringing it back while Centipede was still in the dark place. Gopher had dug a hole and Centipede's ball had rolled into it.

The boy returned to the starting place, and when Centipede saw he had lost, he went no farther but returned and said, "My boy, you have won. Come to my lodge and choose whatever you want for your prize." "No, I don't want to go in there. I want you for my prize." Centipede anxiously said, "Oh, no. I'll give you anything I have." The boy insisted, "I want you." The boy took hold of him and seized him so he could not get away, although Centipede was much bigger. Centipede always had a big fire burning and the boy pulled him toward it. Centipede could not get away. Crow recognized the boy, hopped up to him and said, "I'll help you throw him in. That is what he did to all our people." They threw him in and held him down with the fire tongs he had used on other people until he was burnt up.

Crow then took the boy to Centipede's lodge which was full of hearts and hands. The boy did not touch the hands, but he and Crow carried out the hearts, which were so dried up and shrunken that the two of them could carry them all. As the boy travelled homeward, he buried the hearts in a damp place. The third night he was not far from his home. He went to his sisters and they asked, "Where have you been?" "I have been hunting," he replied. "We are nearly starved." "Never mind, you'll forget that when all our people come back." On the third morning before sunrise, the sisters woke up while their brother pretended to be asleep. They heard laughter and conversation. "Wake up, brother. Hear all the people coming." They were afraid and were going to run away but he said, "Those are our parents and relatives." In this way he got them back.

The Crow now hops because his legs were burnt in Centipede's fire.

The Stars

There were two stars who were brothers. The older one was married. They hunted antelope, tracking and running them down without guns. Once they found one and tracked it. The wife went behind the brother and thought she would fool them. She hid. The two men were far behind. The woman saw an antelope pass her and she followed it. The man said, "We don't catch it like we did before." One of them said, "Perhaps our wife is fooling us." She would always use sinew while the brothers were eating and one of them became suspicious.

The next day they went hunting again and found an antelope track. They were going to follow it differently. One of them said. "Stay here and I'll follow it. I think the antelope will go far off and come back here again." So one of them stayed there while the other kept on tracking the animal. "I'll stay here to see whether it is an antelope or my wife." Soon he saw the antelope come back. He watched it closely and recognized his wife. She wore a hide with a horn on which she carried her baby and she imitated the antelope's hoof marks.

The tracker got there and joined his brother, who said to him, "It is my wife. That is why we didn't catch it." The woman returned about sunset carrying the baby on her back. When she entered she wore neither hide nor horns and looked just like any woman. She said, "Give me the best sinews again. The children play with them and never cry while I am at work." Her husband replied, "I think we'll stay home and not go out. The child will stay with us. You may go for some seeds by yourself."

In the morning the woman left and the men thought they would fool her. They took a log, put moccasins on it, dressed it up like a man, and covered it with a blanket. Before the woman returned, the men went to the water and changed themselves and the baby into antelope to fool her. When she got back, she thought she would get some water since there was none at home. She went to the spring and before getting any water she caught sight of the antelope. She went home to tell her men, but when she took off the robe she saw nothing but a log. Then she thought she would go after the game herself and went back to the spring. The antelope began to run away and she pursued them. Soon she recognized them. "It is my husband and my boy." They kept going. She tried to overtake them but could not do so. She called out, "You had better come back. I am your wife." But they kept on running. Soon she got angry and hit her husband in the neck.

Fly and Coyote's son saw the antelope coming and thought they would kill them, so they hid. Fly shot off an arrow and hit the baby, but did not kill him. Coyote's son tried to shoot but missed. Soon Coyote himself arrived. Fly said, "I shot that one," but Coyote said, "No, my son shot him. I know because that is his arrow. Here is your arrow."

The three stars that are seen with one behind are these four. The husband in front, the boy in the middle, the brother next, and behind them all the woman. The three stars are called Wuyuar and are seen in the winter. The Kusi tawa qari (Pleiades) are sisters of the two brothers in the last story. The two female stars behind the Pleiades were jealous because of a man and fought over him. Plenty of people were around there. The man's mother said, "My boy's knife is under there. Stop fighting, I want to get the knife." All the stars were standing around the fighters. The two jealous women were the two little stars which are seen approaching and receding from each other. This is how people learned to be jealous.

My grandfather thought there was a frog in the moon.

Skunk and Weasel

Skunk and Weasel were brothers-in-law who lived in the Pine-Nut Range. There is a road there that runs to the summit and it is called the Weasel's Road. Weasel had a wife and family and he was always busy getting game for his people. Skunk stayed home all the time. He would threaten to spray the little Weasels with his scent if they didn't give him their food. The little Weasels were getting lean and Weasel and his wife decided that Skunk was the cause of this. So one night they schemed how to get rid of Skunk. The woman said, "Take him to the summit when you hunt and throw him down into the canyon.." "No, I'll tell him to get some arrows tomorrow and have him fix the arrows for himself," said Weasel. Skunk got some cane and put arrowheads on them. He had about a dozen arrows that he put in a quiver. When they were all ready, his sister stealthily pulled one out and put it into her husband's quiver.

The next day Skunk and Weasel went out. They travelled a great distance and caught sight of some deer. Weasel said, "Stay here, and I'll round them up." Weasel set out alone, took the arrow his wife had put in from Skunk's sheaf and shot a deer with it. The rest of the deer were near Skunk and though he shot all his arrows, he didn't hit one. Weasel came and said, "How many have you killed?" "I don't think I have got any of them." "How many arrows did you have?" Skunk counted the arrows and saw that one was missing. Weasel said, "Sometimes you don't remember how many you shoot."

They began to track the deer shot by Weasel and after going some distance they came upon it. Weasel turned it over so that Skunk could see his arrow in it. When Skunk saw it he kicked the deer saying, "I knew that I had shot you. I am sure I shot it. It is my arrow in the deer." He began to skin it. There was a lot of fat in it, and while he was skinning it, Weasel said, "I'll tell you what I do when I kill anything like this. I always have a bite before I take it home. First, build a fire, find a small round stone big enough to hold it in your mouth and heat it red hot."

Skunk built a fire and made a stone red hot. He took some fat and rolled it round the hot stone. "Now," said Weasel, "by doing this you will always be a worker like myself. My grandparents taught me how to do this. That's how I became industrious and why I can support a family. You are a big man, yet you cannot even support yourself. Now, swallow it while it is hot." After Skunk swallowed it, he began to moan. Weasel said, "That's all right. You'll be well pretty soon. I'll go and get a doctor. You stay here."

Instead of going for a doctor, however, he looked for a steep and rocky mountain side. When he had found one, he returned and told Skunk the doctor would not come, but that he would take him there on his back. Weasel took him on his back and set out for the steep mountain. Skunk had his arms round Weasel's neck and Weasel said, "Don't hold me so tight, and put your knees up higher on my back." When he got to the steep place he shook Skunk off. Down went Skunk into the canyon crying, "Soft dirt! Soft dirt!" Weasel cried from the top, "Nothing but rocks! Nothing but rocks!" Skunk landed safely at the bottom of the canyon. Looking up he cried, "You big red-eared Weasel!" Weasel shot all his arrows into him and left him.

Skunk had an uncle named Tokwip. After a long period of time this uncle began to miss him, so he went to the Weasel's place and asked the young ones where their uncle was. They told him they did not know, that he had gone to visit Tokwip. Then Tokwip grew suspicious and looked all over for his nephew until at last he came to the canyon, but saw nothing except Skunk's skin there. Then he knew that Weasel had killed him. Tokwip said, 'I'll get even with Weasel."

Weasel was a great hunter and Tokwip began to hunt him. Sometimes he was close to Weasel, but Weasel always left a short time before Tokwip got near him. One day, however, Tokwip overtook him. Weasel had killed a deer and was preparing to take it home. Tokwip said, "Don't go yet, let us sit down and talk for a while." Then Tokwip said, "What do you say at home when you ask for water?" Weasel said, "I say, 'Give

185

me water and the baby.' " Then Tokwip got up and tried to catch Weasel, but Weasel was too quick and ran away. Tokwip chased him, but when he almost overtook him, Weasel ran into a little hole. Tokwip took his little finger and tore up the earth with it. He caught Weasel, killed him, took out his entrails and scattered them here and there.

Tokwip skinned Weasel, wrapped himself in the skin and went to the place where Weasel had killed a deer. He put the deer on his back. The women in Weasel's family were worried about him because he was coming home so late. Tokwip carried his load to Weasel's home. Weasel always travelled one road and the women could see him coming. They were watching and one of them said, "Here he comes." Another said, "No, it is not Weasel, for he does not carry his load that way."

So they did not stay within the wickiup but went outside as he drew near. Tokwip threw the load off his back and went into the house pretending he was Weasel. Inside he called for water saying, "Give me water and the baby!" But the women were wise and they had already run as soon as he had come in. He repeated his words. At last he got angry, took his arrows and shot them off through the cracks in the walls, but a water jug was hanging there and all the arrows entered its mouth. When he went outside to see where his shots had landed, not a soul was to be seen.

Coyote and Wolf

Coyote and Wolf were brothers. Wolf was the older. Over at Humboldt there was a big cave where Wolf kept all his deer. In those days there were no deer on the mountain, because they were all shut up in that cave. Elk, buffalo, and all of the game were in that cave.

The brothers lived alone a long way from the cave. Early in the morning Wolf went to get some game. He brought just one animal home, maybe an elk, or whatever kind he liked. Coyote asked his brother, "Where did you get that game? How did you hunt that? Every time you go out you get one." At first his brother wouldn't tell him. Then after a while he got angry because Coyote kept asking, so he told him.

Coyote started early in the morning to hunt. He came to the cave and turned all the deer out. When he opened that cave, every kind of game ran out. He tried to shoot one with his bow, but he didn't hit anything. Then Coyote tried to head them back into the cave. He took his fire stick and shot it at a tiny deer and killed it. Wolf saw his brother Coyote. He saw the dust from the running deer and the other game. Wolf was angry, he knew what Coyote had done. When he saw that dust, he lay down.

Coyote left the little deer where he had killed it. He thought he would tell his brother to come and get it. He thought he had killed something big. So he came home and asked his brother to go and bring what he had killed. But Wolf didn't get up, he was very angry. When he didn't move, Coyote himself went back to fetch his game. Then he commenced to cook the meat. He began to laugh. He fell down on his back with his legs in the air and he rolled around. He thought he had caught pretty nice meat. Then Wolf got up and they ate.

Then Coyote asked his brother how he hunted, so Wolf told him. Then Coyote wanted to see how well he could do it. First, Wolf told him how he hunted rabbits. He put two or three piles of sagebrush in a row, and then those piles turned into rabbits. Then he told him how he hunted groundhogs. He went up on the mountain where he could find lots of little rocks. He said, "Rocks, come after me." All those rocks turned into groundhogs when he said that. Then he picked up the groundhogs and took them home.

Now Coyote wanted to hunt the same way as his brother. He tried to hunt rabbits first. He took sagebrush and piled it up, then he looked back, and the piles turned into rabbits. Then he said, "That's an easy way to get rabbits. I'll have to eat these right now, I can bring the next ones home." He ate all the rabbits. Then he tried it again because he wanted some rabbits to take home. He went off a little distance and looked back, but there was nothing but piles of sagebrush. Then Coyote tried groundhog hunting. The first time he said, "Rocks, come after me." Lots of rocks came rolling after him and one big stone fell on him and killed him.

When Coyote didn't come home, Wolf began to look for him. He knew what had happened. When he found his brother under the rock, he kicked him out. He threw him a long way and Coyote came back to life again. Then they went home.

The next morning Wolf told his brother what he had dreamed. He told him, "I dreamed lots of Indians had killed me. You better go get something that we can use to make arrows. When you bring back those sticks, don't get way up on top of the hill." Coyote went to get those sticks and when he had them he went up on the hill, paying no attention to what his brother told him. Some dirt rolled down the hill and he watched. Then some more rolled a little farther. Then Coyote looked the other way, and there he saw lots of Indians. They were the ones his brother dreamed about.

Coyote ran home and said to Wolf, "Your dream was right. There are lots of Indians coming to kill you." Wolf just listened. He said nothing, but kept making arrows. He knew what Coyote had done. If Coyote would do what his brother had told him, those things wouldn't happen. Wolf said, "Cut those sticks." They tied the ends and made points from some hard wood. The feathers on the end were eagle feathers. Wolf just talked, and soon the arrows were finished. When he said, "Now, the bow," the bow flew right toward him and lay right on one side of the arrows. The bow was small at each end and was backed with sinew. Now the bow was finished.

Then Wolf put his brother in his house and shut him in. He told him not to look even though he heard singing and lots of noise. He covered his house all over with dirt and told Coyote not to look even through one crack. "Be sure and don't look," he said. Then Wolf began to fight. He was killing lots of those Indians. His house was built of rye grass and Coyote was inside it. He heard Wolf singing, and he wanted to know what he was doing. He wanted a magic power, too. Coyote asked the Mice to make a hole so he could look through. The Mice made a little hole for him and he could see just a little. Every time his brother shot, lots of Indians were killed. Then he looked at his brother. The minute he saw him, Wolf was shot and killed.

Coyote saw that his brother had been killed and he ran back to his bed.

The Indians who had killed Wolf took his scalp of long hair. Then they tried to look in his house, for they could smell something dead inside. Coyote just made it smell that way so they wouldn't kill him. He didn't want them to bother him. They wondered where Wolf's brother could be and they thought he must have been killed.

Coyote was all by himself now that his brother was killed. He cried every day when he was alone. He decided to follow the Indians who had taken his brother's scalp. He came to the camp they had left. The willows were all red. They had been there a long time before, and the people were all gone now. Coyote travelled a long time — over three nights — and pretty soon he found a fresh green spot.

Pretty soon Coyote saw some Indians. He found a place where women were gathering wood. He saw one woman by herself and asked her, "Where does the chief live?" He found the chief's house and it had Wolf's head hanging in front. Coyote went to the chief and went into his house. There was a fireplace in there and Coyote made the smoke come toward him. He began to cry. Tears ran from his eyes. Then he asked, "Couldn't you let me hold that head?" They gave him the head he wanted. He said, "You have killed a good man. I wish I had been there when you killed him." He acted as though he were not Wolf's brother. Then he looked at the head again and gave it back saying, "That was a good man all right."

Night came and they were going to have a dance. Coyote started to dance. He started circling around. He had a song and he tried to sing it, but he couldn't. Many people were there and they danced all night until it was nearly day.

There were two old women there lying down facing each other. They didn't dance, but they didn't sleep. These two old women were talking about Coyote. They thought Wolf must be his brother. They said, "There were two brothers, that must be one." When day came, everybody went to sleep right where they had been dancing. All were sound asleep. Coyote tried to put the two old women to sleep, but he couldn't.

Then Coyote took his brother's head and ran away with it.
The two old women woke everyone. Coyote headed home with
the head, but they followed him. When they found him, he
threw the head away. When he threw it back, they took it but
didn't harm him. Then Coyote became angry. He said, "I'm
going to kill everyone of those who took my brother's head."
He was looking for a good place and he found two good green
grassy places. He slept in one place. He was by himself, but he
raised many children there. They grew to be warriors and
Coyote told them what to do. He got through talking late in the
evening. The children were going to kill all the people who had
Wolf's head and bring the head to Coyote.

In the meantime, Coyote put on a woman's dress and put a
baby on his back. He went where the people were and
pretended that he was a girl. The people started to dance. Lots
of girls gathered around Coyote and said, "Let's see your baby,
she is crying." He didn't want them to see the baby. "The baby's
father doesn't want anybody to look at his baby," Coyote told
them. Some of the girls said, "What makes you smell like a
man?" "Because I have a man who naturally smells that way,"
Coyote replied.

He wanted all the girls to come with him. He said, "I have
bad magic and many Indians get killed when I'm dancing. We
had better go off some place and sleep." They didn't dance
because they were all gathered around Coyote. They went off
with him to hide somewhere and sleep. Coyote had some kind
of cream to grease his eyes and he gave them some. "Use some
of my grease so you can sleep." After they had used it, Coyote
said, "That was not good grease. Sleep here some place. I'm
going to lay this little niece on this side where you can't hurt
her." Coyote meant the baby. As soon as they lay down, they
went to sleep. It was that grease of Coyote's that made them do
that. When they were all asleep, he tied them together by their
long hair. When he finished, it was daylight.

That's the time Coyote's warriors got there. They began
killing off the Indians. Pretty soon some of Coyote's children
were saying, "Where's the chief? He ought to come here and
help us, here are two we can't kill." Then Coyote came where

they were fighting. "What are these two?" he said. "They are nothing to me." He kicked them with his feet.

He took the head he wanted and started back. He stopped one night where he had raised the children. All the children went away and that was the last of them. Coyote was alone now. He had Wolf's head with him. Every night when he stopped he buried the head in the damp ground. In the morning his brother would be fresher. Now Coyote was nearly home. The next morning he heard his brother's voice, "Black Coyote, get up." That's what he heard it say. He got up and looked around, but he saw no one. He couldn't see his brother, but he heard his voice. Every time he heard it he got up and looked around, but he saw no one. He went back to bed cryng.

Then Coyote reached home. He was still packing his brother's head. The next morning he heard his voice again. Then the next morning he saw his brother with a Wolf blanket over his head. Coyote said, "My brother, my brother, my brother."

That's the end. Coyote caused all that trouble.

Some Adventures of Coyote

Coyote was going along a trail. It was very narrow and he saw many tracks there. He looked up and saw a great big man with a black dog coming toward him. So Coyote sat down and made a white dog with a red eye out of the earth. The man came along the trail and Coyote picked up piles of arrow heads and put them under his shirt. He went toward the man, who was Numuzoho. Numuzoho told Coyote, "Get out of my way, I want to go by." But Coyote stood there and said to him, "Get away and let me pass." Their dogs tried to fight and they howled at each other.

Numuzoho was nicely decorated with beads made from the bones of the people he had eaten many years ago. Coyote wanted to trade beads with him. Numuzoho asked him, "Where are your beads, Coyote?" Coyote still had those arrow points under his shirt. He made them rattle and said, "These are my beads." Numuzoho asked Coyote to dance around so that he could hear the beads rattle. So Coyote danced for him and Numuzoho traded with him.

Coyote told him, "Put your legs on a rock. Lay the arrow heads on top of your legs and mash them with another rock." Then Coyote showed him how to do it. He put the arrow points on his own legs and hit them with a rock. "You see, it didn't hurt me. I am just as before. You can do it, too." So Numuzoho put his legs over the rock as Coyote had told him, and Coyote put points on both his legs. When Coyote was ready to hit him, Numuzoho cried out and put out his hand to shield himself. But Coyote said, "This won't hurt you. You saw me do it."

Numuzoho told Coyote, "There are many people where I come from. Even if they call to you, don't stop, go right on." So Coyote left Numuzoho there. When he had gone a short distance he thought, "I'll look back and see how he is." He looked back. Numuzoho was trying to walk but he couldn't do it with those things on his legs. He fell right down in the same place, because his legs were broken to pieces. He swore at Coyote, "I hope that you will die because of what you did to me!" Numuzoho and his dog died because they had no water to drink. That's the way Coyote got rid of Numuzoho.

Coyote went on his way. Somebody called out, "You are going into a bad place. You might fall in." Coyote went running on. "I'm not afraid, I want to see it myself," he thought. Coyote hauled pitchwood with him. He packed it on his back. He made a rope of sagebrush bark and packed the wood with that. He half believed the warning he had heard. He went on and fell into a great hole. There was a blind person in the hole who was crying. Coyote heard him. The hole had been that way for many years, and Coyote could feel the bones of those who had fallen in. The blind man had just fallen in and wasn't dead yet. Coyote felt around him and found the man's cane. The man was crying because he had lost his cane.

Coyote still had that wood on his back. He put down his pack and then he lay down. He looked up and saw some light. He tried to punch it with his stick. That was the heart of the hole. Then Coyote told the man who was crying, "Stop crying. I have found his heart. We are going to kill him." Coyote was still singing when he said this. Coyote said, "This is my nephew." The man said, "Oh, is that so?" and he came toward Coyote feeling his way. Coyote then drilled fire. He was going to light the pitchwood and burn that heart. The pitchwood burned straight upward and made the gall burst. It exploded and they were thrown up to earth again.

Coyote picked up all the bones and piled them in one place. He made them into persons again, but he killed everyone who was a cannibal. "I wonder if there are any more bones around," Coyote thought. The blind man who was saved said, "There is bad water out there. If you come by the lake, the water will swallow you." That's what he told Coyote.

Coyote travelled on. He was thinking of what he would say to that water. When he came to it, the water began to move. Coyote looked up and the water was ready to swallow him. He looked at that water and then went in up to his hips. Then he jerked back and the water didn't swallow him. Coyote stood up straight and talked to the water. He was standing on the edge of the bank, and the water was moving just a little. He told the water, "I'm going to make a wind come up and throw out the bones of all the people you have eaten. They are going to become alive again. You can't eat me." That's what Coyote told the water.

The wind started to blow. The water was lashed back and forth and the bones were swept out. In a year or so green grass grew between the bones, and they became alive again. The bones that Coyote turned into people moved away, but they left tracks. Coyote came by and saw their trail. He was alone so he camped where they had killed deer and hung the meat to dry. They left scraps of meat in that place. Coyote said, "Oh, my nieces and nephews always treat me so well. They always leave something for me to eat." Coyote was so happy. He went to a shady place and sat down and ate.

He followed their tracks again, but didn't catch up with them. Then he camped alone again. Some noisy little birds called Sanasiwiwi saw Coyote. There was a big willow there and Coyote was looking around for a place to camp. These Birds thought they would stay with him. Before they went to sleep, the Birds took out their eyes and tossed them into the willow tree. Coyote wanted to take out his eyes, but it was very hard to take them out. He worked hard and at last he got them loose. He threw them into the willows. When he woke up he said, "Come on, my nephews, bring me my eyes. I threw them there into the willows." But the Birds wouldn't give them to him. They wanted to play with Coyote's eyes. That is how Coyote lost his eyes.

The Birds were following the same people as Coyote. They saw their trail and the place where they had stopped overnight. They followed them and they took Coyote's eyes with them. Coyote couldn't travel because he had no eyes. He tried to go, but he bumped into sagebrush and fell on the rocks. He fell over and bumped his head. He was getting very thirsty, when he heard a stream running near. He took a stick and felt around with it and found some little yellow flowers. Then he thought, "I guess I'll put them in my eyes. They always close their eyes at night and open them in the daytime." He put them into his eye sockets and he could see again. He drank some water and followed the trail again. Then the yellow flowers wilted and he couldn't see. He was blind again but he went on anyway, following the Birds' trail.

Two women were digging roots. They had never been married and when they found Coyote, he wanted to marry them. The two women saw a deer and they told Coyote, "There's a deer out there." Coyote couldn't see but he said, "I see it." Then he turned the wrong way. The women told him, "You're looking the wrong way, the deer is over there." Coyote said, "You go way around so that the deer will come toward me. I am going to hide and shoot as they pass by." When he heard the deer coming he shot and killed one little fawn.

Then he said to the women, "Go and make a shelter so we can have a fire and a camp." They made a sagebrush enclosure with two openings. Coyote cut that fawn down the top of the head and down the back. "Why do you butcher it that way?" the women asked him. "Because there are two of you. I want to divide it evenly between you," Coyote told them. They cleaned the hide and cut it in two pieces. They planned to leave Coyote as soon as they had tanned that buckskin.

While the two women worked on the hide, Coyote lay down

in camp. He was lying on his side. He put his head in the lap of one of the women and his feet in the lap of the other. Coyote could not see and he had worms in his eyes, but he didn't want his wives to know. One woman was fixing her hair. He tried to hide his face so that she wouldn't see the worms. He went to sleep and the woman found the worms in his eyes. She said to the other one, "You take a stick and put it under his legs. And get lots of ants, we'll put them in his hair." They did that and the ants kept moving in his hair. Some of them bit him and Coyote said, "Don't do that, you are hurting me." His legs were resting on a stick, but he thought they were on his wife's lap.

The two women left Coyote. One left by one door and the other by the other door. They had a fawn's hoof rattle which they shook so that they could keep together. They went toward the rim rock. When Coyote woke up, he sniffed around for their tracks. He followed the younger one and pretty soon he scented both tracks. He followed them straight to the rim rock. The woman said, "If he catches up, we will throw that rattle over the rim. He'll hear and fall over." That's the way they tried to get rid of him. Coyote came up and they threw the rattle over the rim. When Coyote heard it, he ran and fell over the rim.

Then the two women followed the trail. Coyote came to life again and continued to trail them. The women thought they had killed him. They had a grandmother who was pretty old and she walked with a cane. They had left her behind because she was too old to travel. She had a basket on her back and stayed where they had stopped overnight. The two women caught up with her and took turns packing her on their backs.

The Birds who had stolen Coyote's eyes were going to have a big dance. That's why the two women followed them. They left their grandmother and said, "We'll go ahead and see what we can see." One granddaughter came back to see if the old woman was still alive. She told her, "They are going to have a big dance because they have Coyote's eyes. They are over the hill. You keep on following us."

Coyote was still tracking them. Finally he caught up with the old woman. Coyote told her to sit in the shade and rest, because he wanted to question her. "Do you sleep with your granddaughters or by the door?" he asked her. "I tell my granddaughters to bring me water. I never let it get low. I keep it on my back and I say, 'My granddaughters whom men have never seen, give me water.' That's what I say." Then Coyote asked her, "What do you do when you sleep?" She told him, "When I am cold I make a noise in my sleep. Then my granddaughters take me and make me sleep between them. That's why I am not cold in the night."

Then Coyote killed the old woman. He put on her clothes and put her basket on his back. He took her cane and followed the tracks. The two granddaughters were camped apart from the others in a sagebrush enclosure. The girls saw the old lady coming along. Coyote reached the camp and sat down by the door. He had the basket on his back. "My granddaughters whom men have never seen, give me the water," he said. One of the granddaughters ran and got water and gave it to Coyote.

Night came. When they went to bed, Coyote lay at their side. The fire went out and Coyote was cold. He made a noise like the old woman had told him and he made the women sleep so soundly that they knew nothing. The younger sister said, "I don't think this is our grandmother. She smells like a man." She looked at Coyote but she couldn't see his face, so the women got up and left him there. They went to the dance and told him to follow. They said, "I don't think this is our grandmother, she comes too fast. Our grandmother is so old she can hardly move. Look how fast this one comes along." There were lots of hills and everytime Coyote was out of sight he would run and catch up. When he reached the camp, he was worn out. He could hardly walk, so he used his cane with both hands. He sat down and said, "My granddaughters whom men have never seen, get me some water."

They had a sagebrush circle where they were going to dance. There was a pole in the center. That's where they hung Coyote's eyes. The two women heard the drum at sundown and went over there, leaving their grandmother at camp. Everybody was dancing around that pole and one granddaughter said, "Bring that old grandmother over here, maybe she wants to dance, too." So they sent for her. "Come on, grandmother, they want you over there to dance over Coyote's eyes."

So Coyote came. He used his cane and danced around the pole. When he heard the drum beat rapidly he spoke out, "I don't feel very well. I feel like going up in the air." That's how he took his eyes. He jumped in the air and snatched his eyes. Then he jumped over the sagebrush enclosure. One granddaughter said, "That's what I told you. I knew that wasn't our grandmother. That's Coyote."

They followed him. He ran and as he ran he took off the basket and threw it away. Fox was a fast runner and he caught up with Coyote. Coyote told him, "These are my own eyes, nephew, don't bother me." So Fox came back and told his people, "That is Coyote. He has his own eyes, he told me so." They stopped following him.

Coyote went to the water and dampened his eyes. He put them under the ground to freshen them.

REFERENCES CITED

BAHAR, HUSHANG
1955   Pend d'Oreille kinship. Unpublished M.A. thesis, University of Montana, Missoula.

BAKER, PAUL E.
1955   The forgotten Kutenai. Boise: Mountain States Press.

BOAS, FRANZ
1918   Kutenai tales. *Bureau of American Ethnology, Bulletin* 49:1-387.

CAPPANNARI, STEPHEN C.
1950   The concept of property among Shoshoneans. Unpublished Ph.D. dissertation, University of California, Berkeley.

CHAMBERLAIN, A.F.
1893   The coyote and the owl. *Memoirs of the International Congress of Anthropology, Chicago.* pp. 282-284.

1894   A Kootenay legend. *Journal of American Folklore* 7:195-196.

1893-   Notes on the Kootenay Indians. *American Antiquarian*
1895   *and Oriental Journal* 15:292-294; 16:271-274; 17:68-72.

1901a   Kutenai basketry. *American Anthropologist* 11:318-319.

1901b   Kootenay "Medicine-Man." *Journal of American Folklore* 14:95-99.

1901c   Kootenay group-drawings. *American Anthropologist* 3:248-256.

1902   Geographic terms of Kootenay origin. *American Anthropologist* 4:348-350.

1905   The Kootenay Indians. *Annual Archaeological Report, Report of the Minister of Education of Canada.*

1907   Kutenai. *Bureau of American Ethnology, Bulletin* 30(1):
        740-742.

1909   Note sur l'influence exercee sur les Indiens Kitonaga par
        les missionaries catholiques. *Revue des Etudes Ethno-
        graphiques et Sociologiques* 2:155-157.

D'AZEVEDO, WARREN L., *et al.*, eds.
1966   The current status of anthropological research in the
        Great Basin: 1964. *Desert Research Institute, Technical
        Report Series 5-H, Social Science and Humanities
        Publication*, No. 1.

DORN, EDWARD
1966   The Shoshoneans: the people of the Basin-Plateau. New
        York: William Morrow.

DOZIER, JACK
1961   History of the Coeur d'Alene Indians to 1900. Unpub-
        lished M.A. thesis, University of Idaho, Moscow.

DRIVER, HAROLD E.
1961   Indians of North America. Chicago: University of
        Chicago Press.

EGGAN, FRED, ed.
1955   Social anthropology of North American tribes. 2nd
        edition. Chicago: University of Chicago Press.

EWERS, JOHN
1955   The horse in Blackfoot culture. *Bureau of American
        Ethnology, Bulletin* 159.

FOWLER, DON D.
1966   Great Basin social organization. *In* The current status of
        anthropological research in the Great Basin, Warren L.
        d'Azevedo, *et al.*, eds., pp. 57-75.

HAINES, FRANCIS
1938   The northward spread of horses among the Plains
        Indians. *American Anthropologist* 40(3):429-437.

1955   The Nez Perces. Norman: University of Oklahoma Press.

JENNESS, DIAMOND
1932   The Indians of Canada. *National Museum of Canada, Bulletin* 65.

JOSEPHY, A.M., JR.
1965   The Nez Perce Indians and the opening of the northwest. New Haven: Yale University Press.

JUNG, C.G.
1956   On the psychology of the trickster figure. *In* The trickster: a study in American Indian mythology, by Paul Radin, pp. 195-211. New York: Bell Publishing Company.

KELLY, ISABEL T.
1938   Northern Paiute tales. *Journal of American Folklore* 51:363-438.

LOWIE, ROBERT H.
1909   The Northern Shoshone. *Anthropological Papers of the American Museum of Natural History* 2(2):169-306.

1915   Dances and societies of the Plains Shoshoni. *Anthropological Papers of the American Museum of Natural History* 11(10):813-822.

1919   The Sundance of the Wind River Shoshoni and Ute. *Anthropological Papers of the American Museum of Natural History* 16:405-410.

1924a   Notes on Shoshonean ethnography. *Anthropological Papers of the American Museum* 20:185-314.

1924b   Shoshonean tales. *Journal of American Folklore* 37:92-200.

LUNDSGAARDE, HENRY P.
1963   A theoretical interpretation of Nez Perce kinship. Unpublished M.S. thesis, University of Wisconsin, Madison.

MADSEN, BRIGHAM D.
1948   The Bannock Indians in northwest history, 1805-1900. Unpublished Ph.D. dissertation, University of California, Berkeley.

MURDOCK, GEORGE PETER
1960   Ethnographic bibliography of North America, 3rd edition. New Haven: Human Relations Area Files.

1967   Ethnographic atlas. Pittsburgh: University of Pittsburgh Press.

OSWALT, WENDELL
1966   This land was theirs. New York: John Wiley and Sons.

PARK, WILLARD Z.
1937   Paviotso polyandry. *American Anthropologist* 39:366-368.

PHINNEY, ARCHIE
1934   Nez Perce texts. *Columbia University Contributions to Anthropology*, No. 25.

RAY, VERNE F.
1942   Culture element distribution: Plateau (22). *Anthropological Records* 8(2):99-262.

REICHARD, GLADYS A.
1930   The style of Coeur d'Alene mythology. *Proceedings of the International Congress of Americanists* 24:243-253.

1947   An analysis of Coeur d'Alene Indian myths. *Memoirs of the American Folklore Society*, No. 41.

SCHWEDE, MADGE L.
1970   The relationship of aboriginal Nez Perce settlement patterns to physical environment and to generalized distribution of food resources. *Northwest Anthropological Research Notes* 4(2):129-135.

SPENCER, ROBERT F., JESSE D. JENNINGS, *et al.*
1965   *The Native Americans. New York: Harper and Row.*

SPINDEN, HERBERT JOSEPH
1908   The Nez Perce Indians. *Memoirs of the American Anthropological Association*, No. 2.

STEVENS, HAROLD D.
1955   An analysis of Coeur d'Alene Indian-White interrelations. Unpublished M.A. thesis, University of Idaho, Moscow.

STEWARD, JULIAN H.
1936   Shoshoni polyandry. *American Anthropologist* 38:561-564.

1938a   Basin-Plateau aboriginal sociopolitical groups. *Bureau of American Ethnology, Bulletin* 120.

1938b   Lemhi Shoshoni physical therapy. *Bureau of American Ethnology, Bulletin* 119:177-181.

1955   The Great Basin Shoshonean Indians. *In* Theory of culture change, Julian H. Steward, ed., pp. 101-121 Urbana: University of Illinois.

STEWART, OMER C.
1937   Northern Paiute polyandry. *American Anthropologist* 39:368-369.

1939a   The Northern Paiute bands. *Anthropological Records* 2:127-149.

1939b   Washo-Northern Paiute peyotism. *Proceedings of the (fifth) Pacific Science Congress* 6(4):65-68.

1941   Culture element distributions: Northern Paiute (14). *Anthropological Records* 4(3):361-446.

1944   Washo-Northern Paiute peyotism. *University of California Publications in American Archaeology and Ethnology* 40:63-142.

1966   Tribal distributions and boundaries in the Great Basin. *In* The current status of anthropological research in the Great Basin, Warren L. d'Azevedo, *et. al.*, eds., pp. 167-203.

SWANSON, EARL H., JR.

1966   The geographic foundations of desert culture. *In* The current status of anthropological research in the Great Basin, Warren L. d'Azevedo, *et al.,* eds., pp. 137-147.

1970   Languages and cultures of western North America. Pocatello: Idaho State University Press.

TEIT, JAMES A.

1917a   Coeur d'Alene tales. *Memoirs of the American Folklore Society* 1:119-128.

1917b   Pend d'Oreille tales. *Memoirs of the American Folklore Society* 11:114-118.

1930   The Salishan tribes of the western plateaus. *Annual Report of the Bureau of American Ethnology* 45:295-396.

TURNEY-HIGH, HARRY H.

1941   Ethnography of the Kutenai. *Memoirs of the American Anthropological Association,* No. 56.

UNDERHILL, RUTH M.

1941   The Northern Paiute Indians. *Bureau of Indian Affairs, Sherman Pamphlets* 1:1-78.

1953   Red Man's America. Chicago: University of Chicago Press.

1965   Red Man's Religion. Chicago: University of Chicago Press.

VOGT, HANS

1940   The Kalispel language. Oslo: I Kommisjon Hos Jacob Dybwad.

WALKER, DEWARD E., JR.

1964   A survey of Nez Perce religion. New York: Board of National Missions, United Presbyterian Church in the U.S.A.

1966   The Nez Perce sweat bath complex: an acculturational analysis. *Southwestern Journal of Anthropology* 22(2): 133-171.

1967a   Mutual cross-utilization of economic resources in the Plateau: an example from aboriginal Nez Perce fishing practices. *Washington State University, Laboratory of Anthropology, Report of Investigations,* No. 41.

1967b   Nez Perce sorcery. *Ethnology* 6(1):66-96.

1968a   Conflict and schism in Nez Perce acculturation: a study of religion and politics. Pullman: Washington State University Press.

1968b   Some limitations of the renascence concept in acculturation: the Nez Perce case. *In* The American Indian today, Stuart Levine and Nancy Lurie, eds., pp. 149-163. Deland: Everett-Edwards.

1971   The emergent Native Americans. Boston: Little, Brown and Company.

WHITING, BEATRICE B.
1950   Paiute sorcery. New York: *Viking Fund Publications in Anthropology,* No. 15.

WILSON, E.F.
1890   The Kootenay Indians. *Journal of American Folklore* 3:10-12.

- Namrata Dwivedi, my long-time associate and researcher of my novels, who meticulously helped me write the recipes that appear in this book.

- My publisher Krishan Chopra, for his vision...

- Amrita Mukerji for her patience while editing this book and trying out the recipe for 'Miri cha Maas', a family favourite.

- And to all those who asked me, 'How different is Indian Jewish food...?'